ELEGANT FARE
from the Weber Kettle

NEW DIMENSIONS IN OUTDOOR COOKING

by Jane Wood

Photography by Jim Parks

Illustrations by Maggie Swanson

Golden Press/New York
Western Publishing Company, Inc.
Racine, Wisconsin

Jane Wood

Third Printing, 1978

Copyright© 1977 by Weber-Stephen
Products Co., Arlington Heights, Ill.
All rights reserved. Produced in the U.S.A.
Library of Congress Catalog Card Number:
77-73156

weber® is a registered trademark of
Weber-Stephen Products Co.

Dear Outdoor Chef:

These past few years of testing and tasting recipes—of searching out new and unusual dishes, and then enjoying them with friends and family—have been a real joy and adventure for me. Now I'd like to share these barbecue banquets with you. I trust you'll discover, as I did, that they add a new dimension to outdoor living.

For this new cookbook, I've gathered traditional outdoor fare from around the world—Satay from Indonesia, Sosaties from Africa, Easter lamb from Greece, Spiedini from northern Italy, Tandoori Chicken and Peking Duck. You'll find these very special dishes—virtually "born" over the open fire—are ideally suited to the methods and flavors of Weber Kettle cooking.

Here, too, are favorite classics—recipes that bring a new elegance and excitement to alfresco entertaining. Just think of serving Paella Valenciana, Steak au Poivre, Ratatouille and Szechwan Shrimp in the relaxed atmosphere of your own backyard or terrace. To complete the picture, I've also included some great American barbecue specialties, plus a full range of hors d'oeuvres, vegetable dishes and sauces.

If you're a novice, fear not. The recipe card section, a mini cookbook in itself, provides all the basic instructions and preparation tips. These handy punch-out cards can be taken to the beach, to the picnic site, to wherever you choose to use your kettle. (For safekeeping at home, however, be sure to tuck the cards into the special pocket on the inside back cover.) Finally, the charts and introductory material will help you adapt your own favorite recipes to the Weber Kettle.

Please join me in exploring this new wide world of outdoor cooking. Share . . . and enjoy!

Contents

Weber Charcoal and Gas Kettles bring year-round enjoyment of outdoor cooking to the harshest of climates. Designed to cook with the cover on, even when broiling, the kettles need little attention from a hovering chef. Heat from briquettes in the Charcoal Kettle, and from lava rocks in the Gas Kettle, is reflected from the hood, giving the even radiation and fuel economy of an oven while retaining the zesty flavor of barbecue cooking. And simplicity of operation is the key to the outstanding performance of Weber Kettles.

Using Your Weber Charcoal Kettle

To Prepare the Kettle for Use: Position it with 2 vents toward the wind. The leg without a wheel will face toward the wind. Hang the cover by its inside hook on the kettle rim and remove upper grill. Position bottom grill with grid running parallel with the leg facing the wind. Open dampers—3 on the bottom and 1 on the cover—all the way.

How you now prepare your firebed depends on whether you are using the **Direct Heat Method** for fast-cooking foods such as steaks, chops or burgers or the **Indirect Heat Method** for roasts, turkeys, hams or anything that needs slow, even cooking. If you are using the **Direct Heat Method,** proceed with the following steps. If you are using the **Indirect Heat Method,** place the charcoal rails in position (see illustration) before proceeding with instructions.

1. For **Direct Heat Method,** spread briquettes one layer deep over the bottom grill; then scoop them into a heap in the center of the grill. For **Indirect Heat Method,** add required number of briquettes for your series (see Briquette Chart) to either side of the rails.

Briquette Chart

Kettle Series	800	700	300	Smokey Joe
Diameter of grill— inches	26	22¾	18	13½
Briquettes on each side for first hour	30	25	16	9
Briquettes to add to each side every hour	9	8	5	4

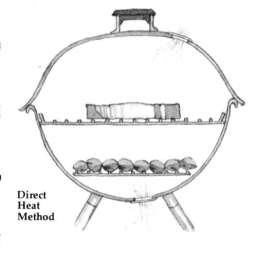

Direct Heat Method

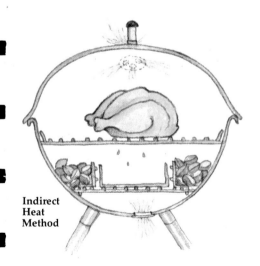

Indirect Heat Method

2. Ignite the fire, using a standard fuel starter or electric starter and following the directions for its use. DO NOT USE GASOLINE, ALCOHOL OR ANY OTHER HIGHLY FLAMMABLE FLUIDS. NEVER ADD STARTER FLUIDS TO HOT OR EVEN WARM COALS.

3. Allow the briquettes to burn with the kettle cover off until a gray ash has formed on the briquettes (25 to 30 minutes).

4. If using **Direct Heat Method,** distribute heaped briquettes evenly over the bottom grill. Replace top grill. If recipe calls for a preheated grill, put the upper grill into position while the coals are heating. Use tongs or heavy mitts to remove and replace it when the briquettes are rearranged. If using **Indirect Heat Method,** place drip pan between charcoal rails. Position top grill with handles directly over the coals to allow the addition of extra charcoal as needed.

5. Place food on grill. When using **Direct Heat Method,** it will be directly over the coals, absorbing their heat. When using the **Indirect Heat Method,** the food will be over the drip pan. Cover kettle with lid vent opposite leg that faces the wind. Cook according to recipe. When cooking by **Indirect Heat Method, add extra charcoal (see Briquette Chart on opposite page) every 60 minutes.**

When food is done, remove it from the grill and cover the kettle. Close all dampers and the fire will go out.

When **Direct** and **Indirect Heat Methods** are used in the same recipe, prepare kettle for **Indirect Heat Method.** Brown meats at either side of the kettle directly over the hot coals with cover off. Turn frequently. Remove and proceed with recipe as directed.

Direct Heat Method

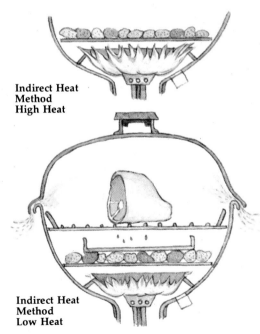

Indirect Heat Method High Heat

Indirect Heat Method Low Heat

Using Your Weber Gas Kettle

To Prepare the Kettle for Use: Hang cover by its inside hook on the kettle rim. Be sure there is an even layer of lava rock across entire bottom grill. If cooking by **Indirect Heat Method (Low Heat),** place a drip pan larger than the piece of meat you are cooking on top of the lava rocks. With COVER OFF, place Burner Control Knob in the Indirect cooking position. Push Heat Control Knob in and turn to High Heat position. Use a match (either paper or wooden) or an electric igniter, and insert into match hole. Place cover on kettle. You are now ready to preheat the grill for cooking by one of three methods: **Direct Heat Method,** used primarily for searing and browning; **Indirect Heat Method (High Heat),** for steaks, chops and burgers; or **Indirect Heat Method (Low Heat),** for roasts and other slow-cooking foods. Instructions for each method follow.

Direct Heat Method: With COVER ON, preheat in the High Heat, Direct position, for 10 minutes. After searing or browning, adjust heat to follow recipe directions for remainder of cooking.

Indirect Heat Method (High Heat): With COVER ON, preheat in the High Heat, Indirect position, for 10 minutes. Remove cover and place food in center of grill. Cover and cook according to recipe directions.

Indirect Heat (Low Heat): With COVER ON, preheat in the High Heat, Indirect position, for 10 minutes. (It is important that the Burner Control Knob be in the Indirect position.) Turn Heat Control to Low position before beginning to cook. Place food on grill directly over drip pan.

When food is cooked, remove from kettle and turn the heat to High Heat, Direct position, for a few minutes to burn all grease from the lava rocks. If drip pan was used, remove before turning up heat.

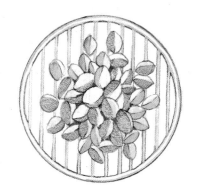

**Briquette Arrangement
for Wok Cooking**

**Briquette Arrangement
for Kebab Cooking**

Special Instructions

Wok Cooking: For charcoal, heap 120 to 150 briquettes in the center of the lower grill, making sure that the wok, when placed in position, nestles directly in them. Ignite briquettes and allow to burn for 25 to 30 minutes or until a gray ash has formed. Set wok in place and proceed as recipe directs. For gas, preheat kettle without upper grill by **Direct Heat Method (High Heat)** for 10 minutes with cover on. Leave at this heat setting, remove cover and place wok in position. Proceed as recipe directs.

Kebab Cooking: For charcoal, use the **Direct Heat Method,** but space the briquettes in a sparse layer so heat is not too intense. For gas, use **Indirect Heat Method, High or Low Heat,** depending on recipe. Use the Heat Control Knob to make sure heat does not become too high.

Meat Thermometer: The Estimated Cooking Times given in this book are just what we say they are—estimated. There is no substitute for a good meat thermometer to tell you when to remove the roast from the grill. We recommend that roasts be allowed to sit off heat for a time specified in each recipe before carving. During this period the roast will continue to cook by its own internal heat, raising the internal temperature as much as 10 to 15 degrees. This explains the discrepancies for temperatures of the degree of doneness between meat thermometers and this book.

Heat Control on Charcoal Kettle: While all vents should be open when starting fire, they may be partially closed during cooking to decrease heat.

Lighting and Preheating Charcoal and Gas Kettles: Both types are ignited with COVER OFF. Replace cover to preheat Gas Kettle only.

Beef

Steak au Poivre

Steak au Poivre is truly elegant fare—especially when served with a creamy mustard sauce and complemented with vegetables and a Caesar salad. To complete the picture, add a hearty red wine.

¼ cup peppercorns
4 beef filet steaks
   (1½ inches thick each)
   Salt
1 shallot, minced
¼ pound butter

Crack the peppercorns on a cloth with a rolling pin or in a mortar with a pestle. Season the steaks with salt; then press an even coating of cracked pepper on each side. Sauté the shallot in butter, in a skillet large enough to hold the steaks in a single layer, until tender. Keep half the shallot butter in the skillet and warm the other half on the other side of the grill for basting. Begin to grill the steaks.

> Grill by **Direct Heat Method** for charcoal, by **Indirect Heat Method (High Heat)** for gas, 10 minutes for rare, 15 minutes for medium. Baste with shallot butter. Turn carefully midway through cooking.

¼ cup cognac
2 teaspoons Dijon mustard
¼ cup heavy cream

When done, place the steaks in the skillet with the shallot butter. Add pre-warmed cognac and flame. Place skillet on grill; move steaks to one side. Add the mustard and cream and stir thoroughly to blend all the sauce ingredients. Remove steaks to a serving platter, pour sauce over the steaks and serve at once. *Serves 4.*

Steak Sandwich

Present this people pleaser on a super-long platter garnished with romaine lettuce, scallions, cherry tomatoes, olives and plenty of pickles.

1 flank steak (2 to 3 pounds)
2 cloves garlic, crushed
  Salt and freshly ground pepper

Use a sharp knife to trim the fibrous outer membrane. Rub the meat with crushed garlic. Season with salt and pepper.

> Grill by **Direct Heat Method** for charcoal, **Indirect Heat Method (High Heat)** for gas, about 5 minutes per side. The outside should be well browned, the inside rare. Medium or well-done flank steak becomes tough.

1 loaf French bread
  Softened butter

Transfer the steak to a platter. Split the bread lengthwise and spread the cut surfaces with a thin layer of butter. Place on the outside edge of the grill to toast lightly. Carve the steak across the grain at a slightly diagonal angle into thin slices. Pile them on bottom half of the bread; replace top and pass with Dijon mustard. *Serves 4.*

Barbecue Sandwich

Before replacing the top slice of bread, pour 1 cup of warmed Smoky Barbecue Sauce (page 60) over the beef.

Spicy Sandwich

¼ cup vegetable oil
2 tablespoons lemon juice
1 tablespoon soy sauce
2 cloves garlic, crushed
  and chopped
3 tablespoons minced scallions
  Few drops of Tabasco sauce

Combine all ingredients and pour over raw meat; refrigerate for several hours. Grill following directions above.

Beef Kebabs

2 pounds beef filet steak
¼ cup peanut oil
¼ cup melted butter
1 clove garlic, crushed

This grilled version of Fondue Bourguignonne combines the unbeatable flavor of hot-coal cooking with the special fun of the fondue tradition.

Trim the beef and cut into 1-inch cubes. Thread onto skewers. Mix oil, butter and garlic in saucepan; keep on side of grill for basting.

> Grill by **Direct Heat Method** for charcoal, by **Indirect Heat Method (High Heat)** for gas. See page 7 for **Special Kebab Instructions.** Turn and baste frequently. Each diner may cook the meat to his own taste.

Serve fondue-style with sauces for dipping (see page 52). *Serves 4.*

Beef Skewers

1 flank steak (2 pounds)
1 recipe Korean Marinade or Teriyaki Marinade (page 61)
1 bunch scallions, cut diagonally into 1½-inch lengths

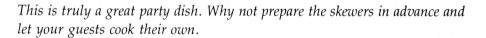

This is truly a great party dish. Why not prepare the skewers in advance and let your guests cook their own.

Semi-freeze the steak for 3 or 4 hours in the freezer. (The meat should be firm-frozen but not rock-hard.) Slice across the grain at a slightly diagonal angle into very thin slices. Mix with the marinade of your choice and refrigerate for 1 to 2 hours. Weave loosely, with scallions, onto skewers.

> Grill by **Direct Heat Method** for charcoal, by **Indirect Heat Method (High Heat)** for gas. See page 7 for **Special Kebab Instructions.** Grill for 3 or 4 minutes per side. The meat is most tender when rare.

Serve as part of an appetizer ensemble or on their own. *Serves 4.*

Liver with Bacon and Onions

I've converted many skeptics into liver-lovers with this dish, myself included. For best flavor, liver should be well browned outside, slightly pink inside.

2 pounds calf's liver (cut 1 inch thick)
¼ cup olive oil
2 cloves garlic, crushed
Freshly ground pepper
Grilled Onions (below)
4 to 6 slices bacon

Combine the sliced liver with the oil, garlic and a sprinkling of black pepper. Refrigerate for 3 hours, stirring occasionally. Start the onions 15 minutes before you are ready to begin the liver. When the onions are turned, place the bacon on the grill, topping each strip with a slice of liver.

> Grill by **Direct Heat Method** for charcoal, by **Indirect Heat Method (High Heat)** for gas. After 5 minutes, separate and turn the liver and bacon and cook apart another 5 minutes. Top the liver slices with bacon and cook for a final 5 minutes.

Serve with Grilled Onions (below).   *Serves 4 to 6.*

Grilled Onions

2 Spanish onions, cut in ½-inch-thick slices
Melted butter or oil

Push a small skewer into the side of each slice and through it for easy turning and to hold the rings together. Brush with melted butter.

> Grill by **Direct Heat Method** for charcoal, by **Indirect Heat Method (High Heat)** for gas, for 30 minutes. Turn after 15 minutes. The rings should be just tender, not limp.

These go well with burgers and grilled or roasted meats. *Serves 4 to 6.*

Sweetbreads en Brochette

This French specialty is made from the thymus gland, located in the throat of the calf. Its subtle flavor has made the sweetbread a delicacy for centuries.

1 pound veal sweetbreads
½ pound mushroom caps
8 cherry tomatoes, blanched and peeled
Melted butter

To prepare the sweetbreads for the grill, soak them in several changes of ice water for 2 or 3 hours. Pick off as much of the membrane as possible; then simmer in acidulated water (1 quart water, 2 tablespoons lemon juice, 2 teaspoons salt) for 10 minutes. Cool quickly under cold running water. Arrange them on a plate, place another plate on top and weight the top plate to firm and flatten the sweetbreads and to squeeze out any excess water. Refrigerate for 2 to 3 hours.

Cut the sweetbreads into 1-inch chunks. Alternate on 4 skewers with the mushroom caps and tomatoes.

Grill by **Direct Heat Method** for charcoal, by **Indirect Heat Method (High Heat)** for gas, for 10 minutes. Turn frequently, basting with melted butter.

Serve with lemon wedges and Maître d'Hôtel Butter (below). *Serves 2.*

Maître d'Hôtel Butter

½ cup butter, softened
1 tablespoon chopped parsley
¼ teaspoon salt
Freshly ground pepper
1 teaspoon lemon juice

Cream all ingredients until fluffy.

Beef Bird Casserole

This stuffed bacon-wrapped beef roll comes from northern Italy, where it is known as Messicani alla Milanese. It is one of my favorite all-around recipes.

12 slices (¼x4 to 5 inches each)
    beef round or veal leg
 2 tablespoons butter
 1 medium onion, chopped
 1 clove garlic, minced
 6 medium mushrooms, chopped

¼ pound lean ground pork
1½ cups dry bread crumbs
 2 tablespoons milk
¼ cup melted butter
 2 eggs
 3 tablespoons chopped parsley
½ teaspoon grated lemon peel
 1 teaspoon salt
12 slices bacon

2 cups beef stock or 1½ cups beef
   stock and ½ cup red wine

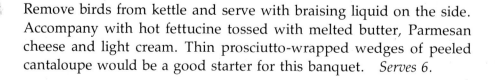

Flatten the meat slices between 2 sheets of waxed paper with a heavy mallet until each slice is as thin as possible without tearing the meat. Heat the butter in a skillet; sauté the onion and garlic until the onion is limp and translucent. Add the mushrooms and cook, stirring, 3 minutes. Empty the contents of the pan into a mixing bowl.

Using the same pan, cook the pork until it is white and crumbly. Add the pork, bread crumbs, milk, butter, eggs, parsley, lemon peel and salt to the mushrooms and onions; stir until blended. Spread 2 to 3 tablespoons filling on each meat slice to within ½ inch of the edge. Roll the meat and wrap each bird spirally with a strip of bacon. Secure the bacon ends with wooden picks.

Cook by **Indirect Heat Method** for charcoal, by **Indirect Heat Method (Low Heat)** for gas. Brown the beef birds over the coals on either side of the grill for about 15 minutes. Watch for flare-ups. Transfer the beef birds to a shallow casserole. Add beef stock. Bake for 1 hour.

Remove birds from kettle and serve with braising liquid on the side. Accompany with hot fettucine tossed with melted butter, Parmesan cheese and light cream. Thin prosciutto-wrapped wedges of peeled cantaloupe would be a good starter for this banquet. *Serves 6.*

Stuffed Peppers and Onions

Delicious, economical and quick and easy, too. The meat mixtures for Mexican Burgers (page 16) and Chinese Burgers (page 18) also make good stuffing for peppers or onions.

3 large onions
3 large green peppers
1 pound lean ground beef
1 can (10½ ounces) tomato puree
⅓ cup chopped parsley
½ cup long grain rice
1½ teaspoons salt
  Freshly ground pepper
1 tomato, cut in 6 slices
2 cups chicken stock

Peel the onions and trim the ends. Cut the onions in half crosswise and punch out the center sections to form 6 onion cups. Cut the centers into ½-inch slices; set aside. Slice the peppers in half lengthwise; remove the ribs and seeds. Combine the ground beef, ¼ of the can of tomato puree, parsley, rice, salt and pepper. Stuff the pepper and onion cups. Place an onion slice (cut from the onion centers) on top of each pepper cup, and a tomato slice on top of each onion cup. Arrange the peppers and onions checkerboard fashion in a 13x9x2-inch baking pan. Add the chicken stock; pour the remaining tomato puree over the peppers and onions. Cover with foil.

Cook by **Indirect Heat Method** for charcoal, by **Indirect Heat Method (Low Heat)** for gas, for 1 hour. Add water or stock to the pan as needed to maintain the initial liquid level.

Serves 6.

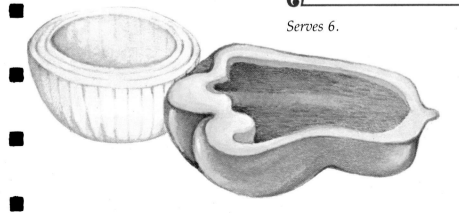

Mexican Burgers

1 pound ground beef
½ cup crushed corn chips
⅓ cup evaporated milk
2 tablespoons minced onion
1 teaspoon Worcestershire
   sauce

A complementary contrast between the creaminess of guacamole and the toothsome texture of corn chips. This recipe makes a great meat loaf, too.

Thoroughly mix the ground beef, chips, milk, onion and Worcestershire sauce with a wooden spoon. Shape into 4 patties.

> Grill by **Direct Heat Method** for charcoal, by **Indirect Heat Method (High Heat)** for gas, about 5 minutes per side or until nicely browned and cooked through. Turn once.

Serve topped with Guacamole (below). If using toasted buns, halve the Guacamole recipe.   *Serves 4.*

Guacamole

1 clove garlic, cut in half
2 large avocados
2 tablespoons lemon or lime juice
2 tablespoons minced onion
1 tomato, peeled, seeded, finely
   chopped and drained
   Tabasco sauce or cayenne
   pepper to taste
½ teaspoon salt
   Mayonnaise

This also makes a great appetizer dip for corn chips or raw vegetables.

Rub a serving bowl with the cut sides of the garlic. Mash the avocados in the bowl with a fork, blending in lemon juice. Stir in the onion, tomato, Tabasco and salt. Smooth the mixture into a mound and spread a thin layer of mayonnaise over the exposed surface to prevent discoloration. Just before serving, stir in the mayonnaise. *Makes about 2 cups.*

Stuffed Bacon Busha Burgers

2½ pounds lean ground beef
1 tomato, cut into 6 slices
6 thin slices onion
6 slices cheese (Swiss, Cheddar, mozzarella or your favorite)
6 slices bacon

Somehow stuffed "anything" is just a little bit special. The combinations are endless. Here are some of my favorites. Try some of your own.

Make 12 patties, each about 5 inches across and ½ inch thick. Sandwich a tomato, onion and cheese slice between 2 patties and carefully seal the edges. Wrap a slice of bacon around the outside edge of each burger; secure with a wooden pick.

Grill by **Direct Heat Method** for charcoal, by **Indirect Heat Method (High Heat)** for gas, for 5 to 6 minutes per side for medium. When the first side has browned, turn and brown the other side.

A crisp salad and a fresh green vegetable would finish this meal nicely. *Serves 6.*

Stuffing Variations: Sliced green olives; sautéed sliced mushrooms; sliced avocado; sliced marinated artichoke hearts; egg salad; chopped pickle.

Chinese Burgers

East meets West in this beef mixture that not only makes great hamburgers, but also makes a significant meat loaf and stupendous stuffed peppers.

1 **pound lean ground beef or pork**
¼ **cup fresh bean sprouts**
3 **tablespoons minced bamboo shoots**
4 **mushrooms, minced**
2 **scallions, minced**
2 **thin slices gingerroot, minced**
2 **tablespoons dry sherry**
2 **tablespoons soy sauce**
½ **teaspoon sugar**
1 **teaspoon cornstarch Freshly ground pepper**

Combine all ingredients. Shape into 4 patties.

> Grill by **Direct Heat Method** for charcoal, by **Indirect Heat Method (High Heat)** for gas, about 5 minutes per side for beef, 8 minutes per side for pork. Turn carefully.

Serve with Sweet-Sour Apricot Sauce (below). *Serves 4.*

Sweet-Sour Apricot Sauce

½ **cup apricot preserves**
3 **tablespoons vinegar (or to taste)**

Combine ingredients in blender jar. Turn the blender quickly on and off several times to puree the preserves and blend the flavors.

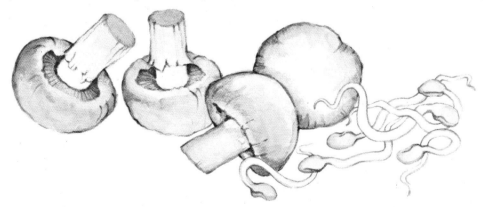

Cheese Burgers

There are two secrets to these extraordinarily good burgers: Freshly ground chuck or round that is not too fat or too lean, and light handling of the meat.

1½ **pounds lean ground beef**
½ **teaspoon sweet basil**

Shape the beef quickly and lightly into four ¾-inch-thick patties. Sprinkle with basil.

4 **slices imported Swiss cheese**

> Grill by **Direct Heat Method** for charcoal, by **Indirect Heat Method (High Heat)** for gas, for about 4 minutes per side. Turn midway in cooking and place a slice of cheese on cooked side.

Serve on hard rolls topped with Grilled Onions (page 12).   *Serves 4.*

Beef Olive Loaf

The coals do as much for meat loaf as they do for a juicy hamburger. Or try stuffing a meat loaf, as with Stuffed Bacon Busha Burgers (page 17).

2 **pounds lean ground beef**
1 **pound lean ground pork**
2 **cloves garlic, minced**
1 **onion, finely chopped**
1 **green pepper, seeded and chopped**
½ **cup sliced green olives**
½ **cup bread crumbs**
2 **eggs**
½ **teaspoon thyme**
1 **teaspoon salt**
½ **teaspoon freshly ground pepper**
6 **slices bacon**

Combine all ingredients except the bacon in a large bowl. Blend with a wooden spoon. Form into a loaf and place in a baking pan. Lay the bacon slices across the top of the loaf.

> Cook by **Indirect Heat Method** for charcoal, by **Indirect Heat Method (Low Heat)** for gas, for 1½ hours. See **Briquette Chart**, page 4, for extra coals.

Pork

Pineapple-Pork Kebabs

2½ to 3 pounds pork,
    preferably fresh ham
  1 cup sugar
  2 teaspoons salt
  2 tablespoons soy sauce
  2 eggs
  3 small onions
  2 green peppers
    Cornstarch
1½ cups pineapple chunks

Peanut oil

The flavors of onion, peppers, pineapple and pork combine and blend beautifully. I've added a marinade, the best pork marinade ever encountered, that transforms this simple dish into a specialty. Since these kebabs are true party pleasers, be sure to try them as hors d'oeuvres sometime.

Trim away any fat or gristle from the meat and cut into 1-inch cubes. Combine the sugar, salt, soy sauce and eggs. Stir in pork and refrigerate several hours, stirring occasionally. Meanwhile, cut the onions in half and peppers into 1-inch-square pieces. Remove pork from marinade and dredge in cornstarch. Skewer, alternating with onion, green pepper and pineapple chunks.

Grill by **Direct Heat Method** for charcoal, by **Indirect Heat Method (Low Heat)** for gas. See page 7 for **Special Kebab Instructions.** Cook for 15 to 20 minutes or until peppers and onions are tender and pork is thoroughly cooked. Turn frequently, basting with peanut oil after first 5 minutes.

Pass sweet-and-sour sauce at the table, if desired. Rice garnished with red and green peppers and salad are excellent accompaniments. Offer fresh fruit either during or after the main course. *Serves 4 to 6.*

Indonesian Satay

The satay street vendors are more common in Bangkok than the hot dog men on the South Side of Chicago.

3 pounds boneless lean pork

¼ cup peanut oil
¼ cup soy sauce
1 tablespoon chopped onion
1 clove garlic, crushed
1 teaspoon sugar
⅛ teaspoon curry powder

Peanut oil

Cut the pork into 1x4x¼-inch strips.

Combine the ¼ cup peanut oil with the soy sauce, onion, garlic, sugar and curry powder. Stir in the pork and refrigerate for 1 to 2 hours. Stir occasionally. Thread the pork strips onto thin skewers.

> Grill by **Direct Heat Method** for charcoal, by **Indirect Heat Method (High Heat)** for gas. See page 7 for **Special Kebab Instructions.** Cook for 6 to 10 minutes. Turn and baste frequently with peanut oil.

Accompany with Peanut Sauce (below).   *Serves 4 to 6.*

Peanut Sauce

½ cup shredded coconut
¾ cup hot milk
2 tablespoons butter
½ teaspoon curry powder
1 onion, finely chopped
½ teaspoon minced gingerroot
1 clove garlic, minced
½ cup crushed pineapple
3 tablespoons crunchy peanut butter
2 tablespoons sugar
½ teaspoon salt
Freshly ground pepper
½ cup chicken stock

Add the shredded coconut to the hot milk and soak for 30 minutes. Heat the butter in a skillet. Add curry powder and cook, stirring, for 1 to 2 minutes. Add onion, gingerroot and garlic and sauté, stirring, for 5 minutes. Add shredded coconut and milk and remaining ingredients; stir to blend. Cook, covered, stirring occasionally, for 20 minutes. Serve warm.   *Makes about 2½ cups sauce.*

Sosaties

1½ pounds boneless lean
   pork shoulder or loin
½ cup dried apricots

1 pound small white onions
2 tablespoons peanut or
   vegetable oil

1 teaspoon curry powder
1 teaspoon peppercorns
1 cup cider vinegar
1 tablespoon brown sugar
1 cup dry white wine
2 tablespoons apricot jam

Salt and freshly ground
pepper

Take advantage of African expertise in open-coal cooking and share with me this offering from an exchange student who was also an accomplished cook.

Cut pork into 1-inch cubes; set aside in large bowl. Soak apricots in warm water until softened; drain and add to pork.

Trim onion ends and peel. Sauté in oil, stirring frequently, for 10 minutes. Remove the onions and add to pork. (Do not drain pan.)

Add the curry powder and peppercorns to the pan in which the onions were cooked. Sauté for 1 to 2 minutes to take the raw taste from the curry. Add vinegar, brown sugar, wine and jam. Stir and cook just to boiling. Pour marinade over the pork, apricots and onions and refrigerate for 24 hours. Pour marinade into small saucepan and place on side of grill.

Alternately thread meat, apricots and onions on skewers; sprinkle with salt and pepper. *Serves 4.*

Grill by **Direct Heat Method** for charcoal, by **Indirect Heat Method (Low Heat)** for gas. See page 7 for **Special Kebab Instructions.** Cook for 30 minutes or until pork is thoroughly cooked. Turn frequently, basting with marinade.

Stuffed Pork Loin Roast

This is the stout, hearty fare that has brought fame to the tables of Germany. The presentation is impressive, with the roast fanning out beautifully.

1 boned, rolled pork loin
(4 pounds), trimmed
Pork Stuffing (below)

Using a sharp knife, slice the roast halfway down at 1-inch intervals. Continue each slice to form deep pockets, leaving a 1-inch wall on the sides and bottom.

Pork Stuffing

  3 tablespoons butter
  2 medium onions, chopped
  2 apples, cored, peeled and chopped
½ cup chopped boiled ham
¾ cup chopped ripe olives
½ cup chopped walnuts
  1 cup soft bread crumbs
½ teaspoon salt
¼ teaspoon thyme
  3 tablespoons melted butter

Heat the butter in a skillet and sauté the onions, stirring occasionally, until they are limp and transparent. Add the apples and cook 1 minute more. Combine with the remaining ingredients and mix well.

Generously stuff the roast, then tie at 1-inch intervals around the outside to hold the roast together (see illustration).

> Cook by **Indirect Heat Method** for charcoal, by **Indirect Heat Method (Low Heat)** for gas, for 1½ to 2 hours or until meat thermometer buried halfway in the *center pork slice* registers 170°. See **Briquette Chart**, page 4, for extra coals.

Remove roast from kettle and allow to stand 10 minutes before carving. Remove the strings and slice through the meat between pockets to yield individually stuffed chop portions. Roast Potatoes (page 78) and a fresh green vegetable would be nice additions. *Serves 8.*

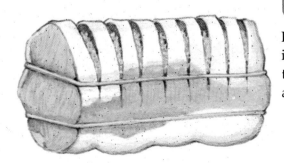

Savory Pork Roast

The pork roast comes courtesy of the great Cajun cooks down Louisiana way.

1 pork loin roast (3½ to
   4 pounds)
4 to 6 cloves garlic, slivered
1 teaspoon rosemary
1 teaspoon salt

Wipe the roast with a damp cloth. Make tiny ¼-inch-wide and 1-inch-deep slits over the surface of the roast, about 1 inch apart, with the tip of a thin-bladed knife. Stuff each with a sliver or two of garlic. Crush the rosemary leaves and rub the salt and rosemary over the surface of the roast.

Cook by **Indirect Heat Method** for charcoal, **Indirect Heat Method (Low Heat)** for gas, for about 20 to 35 minutes per pound or until an internal temperature of 160° has been reached. The thermometer should be placed in the center of the thickest portion of meat, not touching fat or bone. See **Briquette Chart,** page 4, for extra coals.

Allow the roast to stand for 20 minutes before carving so that the juices will settle. Delicious accompanied with Banana-Stuffed Sweet Potatoes (page 76). *Serves 6 to 8.*

Pork Steaks

Ideally, pork steaks for barbecuing should be cut from a fresh ham. These steaks are delicious plain from the grill or glazed.

3 to 3½ pounds pork steaks,
  1 inch thick
Garlic powder
Salt and freshly ground pepper
Rosemary or thyme

Wipe the steaks with a damp cloth. Sprinkle generously with garlic powder, salt, pepper and crushed rosemary leaves or thyme.

> Grill by **Direct Heat Method** for charcoal, by **Indirect Heat Method (Low Heat)** for gas, for about 15 minutes per side.

Fresh garlic bread and a combination vegetable salad makes this a quick-and-easy company dinner.   *Serves 4.*

Barbecue Glaze Sauce

½ cup soy sauce
¾ cup catsup
¾ cup honey
 3 cloves garlic, minced
½ teaspoon Tabasco

Combine ingredients and mix well. Prepare and begin to grill the steaks as indicated above. After 5 minutes per side, begin basting and turning the steaks until they are browned, glazed and thoroughly cooked. Serve with remaining sauce on the side.

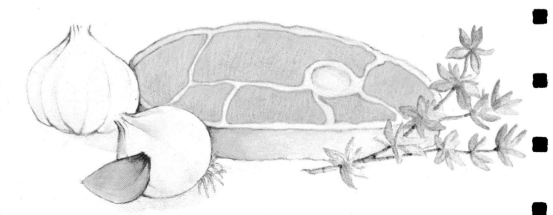

Sausages on the Grill

For simple, hearty fare, perfect for crisp autumn get-togethers, serve a mixed grill of international sausages with a variety of good bakery breads, mustards and deli dill pickles.

Bratwurst: Fresh or precooked German sausage made with veal and pork.

Pork Sausage: Fresh American sausage made with pork and pork fat.

Italian Sausage: Fresh hot or mildly seasoned pork sausage; "pizza sausage."

German Sausage: Fresh pork sausage made in continuous ropes; bake for best flavor.

Frankfurters: Cooked blend of pork and beef; Kosher franks are all beef.

Kielbasa or Polish Sausage: Fresh, cooked or smoked pork sausage, sometimes made with veal or beef. Check label for cooking instructions.

Knackwurst: Cooked, chunky German frank highly seasoned with garlic.

Thuringer: Smoked, unsmoked, fully cooked and occasionally fresh German sausage of pork and veal. Check label for cooking instructions.

Many of our supermarkets now offer a fine selection of fresh sausages. The most common ones found are listed in the column to the left. Check around town for a good sausage selection. You'll need ⅓ to ½ pound per serving. Here are 2 methods of preparation for uncooked sausages and 1 for fully cooked sausages.

Simmered and Grilled: Simmer, covered, on top of stove in beer, white wine or water to cover, 20 minutes for 1- to 1½-inch-thick sausages, 10 minutes for finger-thick sausages. Drain, brush with butter and grill by **Direct Heat Method** for charcoal, by **Indirect Heat Method (High Heat)** for gas, until browned.

Baked: Place sausages in baking pan and bake by **Indirect Heat Method** for charcoal, by **Indirect Heat Method (Low Heat)** for gas, 45 minutes for 1- to 1½-inch-thick sausages, 25 minutes for finger-thick sausages.

For Fully Cooked Sausages: Brush with butter and grill by **Direct Heat Method** for charcoal, by **Indirect Heat Method (High Heat)** for gas, until warmed through and browned.

Lamb

Stuffed Lamb

Serve this gourmet treat with a platter of delicate vegetables and fresh spinach salad with a touch of lemon and oil. Simply wonderful!

1 leg of lamb (6 pounds), boned
Lamb Stuffing (below)
2 cloves garlic, slivered
½ teaspoon crushed rosemary
1 teaspoon salt
Freshly ground pepper
½ cup Dijon mustard
2 cups lamb stock or 1 cup
  red wine and 1 cup water

Ask your butcher to bone the lamb for stuffing. Also have him trim the fell (outside membrane) and remove the fat. Prepare stuffing and stuff the cavity of the lamb; skewer and lace the ends closed. Puncture the meat, here and there, with the tip of a sharp paring knife and insert the garlic slivers. Rub the stuffed leg with rosemary, salt and pepper, then brush on a generous coating of mustard. Pour the liquid into the drip pan.

> Cook by **Indirect Heat Method** for charcoal, by **Indirect Heat Method (Low Heat)** for gas, for 1½ to 2 hours or until meat thermometer placed in the center of the thickest portion of meat registers 140° for medium rare, 150° for medium. See **Briquette Chart**, page 4, for extra coals.

1 tablespoon Dijon mustard

Allow roast to stand for 20 minutes before carving. Strain the pan juices and blend in the mustard. Serve with lamb.   *Serves 8.*

Lamb Stuffing

¾ cup dry bread crumbs
3 tablespoons milk
2 tablespoons butter, softened
½ pound lean ground lamb
2 tablespoons minced scallions
1 clove garlic, minced
¼ teaspoon ground rosemary
  Salt and freshly ground pepper

Moisten the bread crumbs with the milk, and cream with softened butter. Add remaining ingredients and knead to mix thoroughly.

Butterflied Leg of Lamb

Lamb is best eaten rare or medium rare like good roast beef. The cooking time is short and you have no bone to contend with. Give it a try.

1 **leg of lamb (6 pounds)**
2 **cloves garlic**
2 **teaspoons salt**
1 **teaspoon freshly ground pepper**
1 **tablespoon crushed rosemary**
   Olive oil

Remove the lamb's fibrous outer membrane with a knife. Make a deep cut lengthwise along the bone; cut and scrape the meat from the bone and "butterfly," or flatten, the meat out into a thick steak. Crush, peel and mince the garlic and rub it into the meat along with the salt, pepper and rosemary. Pat olive oil onto the lamb and allow to stand at room temperature for 30 minutes.

Grill by **Direct Heat Method** for charcoal, by **Indirect Heat Method (High Heat)** for gas, for approximately 15 minutes per side for medium rare, 25 minutes per side for well done. Check with meat thermometer in thickest part to be sure (140° medium rare, 160° well done). Baste with oil.

Marinated Variation: Rub the meat with salt, pepper and garlic as above. Combine ½ teaspoon thyme, ½ teaspoon oregano, 3 tablespoons red wine vinegar, ½ cup red wine, ½ cup olive oil and 1 bay leaf. Pour the marinade over the meat and refrigerate for 24 hours, turning the meat occasionally. Grill as above, basting with marinade. Serve with a sauce made of ½ cup melted butter flavored with the juice of 1 lemon.

Double Lamb Chops

These luscious lamb chops are appropriate for the most luxurious dining.

4 double-rib lamb chops, about 2½ inches thick
2 tablespoons olive oil
8 to 10 cloves garlic, crushed
Juice of 1 lemon
Salt and freshly ground pepper

Ask the butcher to French (trim) the bone ends and supply the paper frills that cap the bones after cooking. Brush the chops with olive oil and spread with crushed garlic. Sprinkle with lemon juice, salt and pepper and let stand for 1 to 2 hours.

> Grill by **Direct Heat Method** for charcoal, by **Indirect Heat Method (High Heat)** for gas, for 8 minutes per side for rare, 10 minutes per side for medium rare.

Cap bone ends with paper frills. Serve chops on warm plates topped with Mustard Butter (below). Accompany with Grilled Eggplant (page 75). *Serves 4.*

Mustard Butter

½ cup butter, softened
1 tablespoon Dijon mustard
½ teaspoon lemon juice
1 clove garlic, pressed
Salt and freshly ground pepper

Cream butter with remaining ingredients until fluffy. Serve at room temperature. *Makes ½ cup.*

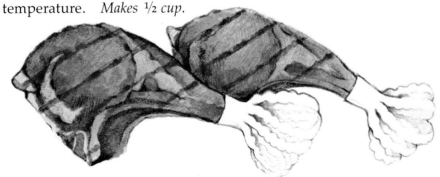

Turkish Tacos

What we have here is a crazy mix of the Greek gyros sandwich, the American hot dog, the Turkish shish kebab and the Mexican taco.

1½ **pounds lean ground lamb**
1 **small onion, minced**
3 **egg yolks**
⅛ **teaspoon saffron soaked in 1 teaspoon water**
⅛ **teaspoon cinnamon**
⅛ **teaspoon cumin**
1 **teaspoon salt**
  Freshly ground pepper
2 **green peppers, cut into 12 1-inch squares**
6 **pieces of Pita bread**

Combine the lamb, minced onion, egg yolks, saffron, cinnamon, cumin, salt and pepper in a bowl. Mix thoroughly. Form the meat mixture into 6 "sausages," 5 to 6 inches long. Skewer a green pepper square, a lamb "sausage" and another green pepper square. Press the peppers into the meat to be sure the lamb mixture is securely molded to the skewer. Continue until all the "sausages" are carefully skewered.

Grill by **Direct Heat Method** for charcoal, by **Indirect Heat Method (High Heat)** for gas, for 15 to 20 minutes. Wrap the Pita bread in foil (2 pieces per package) and heat on the edge of the grill during the last 10 minutes of cooking time. Turn packages after 5 minutes.

To serve, place a skewered "sausage," with peppers, on each piece of Pita bread. Spread with Yogurt Sauce (page 59), garnish with sliced onion and tomato, fold up the sides and dig in.   *Serves 6.*

Yogurtlu Kebabs

Skewer cooking was born centuries ago on the swords of Turkish warriors trying to get a good hot meal without too much bother.

2 pounds boneless lamb shoulder
    or leg
2 tablespoons olive oil
1 small onion, grated
1 clove garlic, crushed
½ cup unflavored yogurt
½ teaspoon salt
    Freshly ground pepper

Paprika
Sesame seed

Trim off any gristle and cut the lamb into 1-inch cubes. Combine the remaining ingredients and blend with a whisk. Add the lamb chunks and stir to coat each piece. Cover tightly and marinate in the refrigerator overnight.

Skewer the meat chunks, pushing them tightly against one another. Lightly sprinkle each skewer with paprika and sesame seed.

> Grill by **Direct Heat Method** for charcoal, by **Direct Heat Method (High Heat)** for gas, for about 10 minutes, turning frequently. Meat should be well browned on the outside and pink and juicy on the inside.

Ratatouille (page 73), cooked beforehand and kept warm while kebabs are grilled, makes this meal party fare. *Serves 4 to 6.*

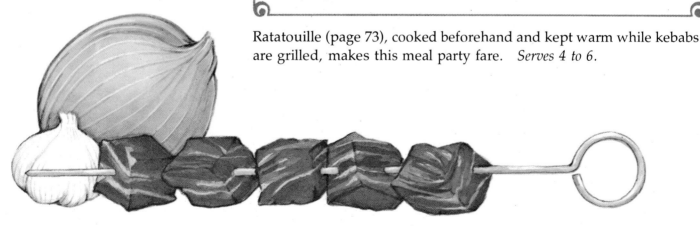

Poultry

Stuffed Roast Chicken

We enjoy this Stuffed Roast Chicken so much that one bird is not enough. If the second chicken is not consumed on the spot, serve it cold another day and dare anyone to call it a leftover. Extra stuffing turns mushroom caps into a surprise hors d'oeuvre.

1 roasting chicken (3 pounds)
6 slices bacon
2 tablespoons butter
1 medium onion, finely chopped
2 chicken livers
¾ cup dry bread crumbs
½ cup walnuts, chopped
3 tablespoons chopped parsley
2 eggs
¼ teaspoon salt
Freshly ground pepper
⅛ teaspoon cinnamon

Wash the chicken inside and out; drain. Chop 3 slices of bacon and fry until crisp. Remove the bacon with a slotted spoon and drain. Add the butter and chopped onion to the pan and sauté until the onions are translucent and just cooked through. Chop the livers and combine thoroughly with the onions and pan juices, crisp bacon and remaining ingredients. Stuff the chicken, sew the cavities closed and truss the bird tightly (see page 36). Lay the remaining 3 slices of bacon over the breast, lengthwise, to baste during cooking.

> Cook by **Indirect Heat Method** for charcoal, by **Indirect Heat Method (Low Heat)** for gas, for approximately 2 hours or until juices run clear when thigh is pierced. See **Briquette Chart**, page 4, for extra coals.

Extra stuffing goes into mushroom caps (below).   *Serves 4.*

Stuffed Mushroom Caps

Spoon excess stuffing into mushroom caps. Wrap with partially cooked bacon and skewer loose ends.

> Grill by **Direct Heat Method** for charcoal, by **Indirect Heat Method (High Heat)** for gas, until bacon is browned and crispy.

Tandoori Chicken

This Indian dish is another international specialty unalterably linked to open-coal cooking. Despite the spices, it is surprisingly mild.

1 roasting chicken (3 pounds)
1 small onion
4 cloves garlic
½-inch piece of gingerroot,
   peeled and chopped
1 teaspoon cumin
1 teaspoon coriander
½ teaspoon chili powder
½ teaspoon cinnamon
1 teaspoon salt
½ cup yogurt
   Juice of 1 lemon
   Tandoori Basting Sauce
   (below)

Pierce the chicken, all around, with a fork. Grind the onion, garlic and ginger together in a grinder or blender. Add seasonings and mix thoroughly. Beat the yogurt in a bowl until smooth; blend in the spice paste and lemon juice. Rub the mixture into the chicken and let it marinate in the refrigerator for at least 4 hours or overnight.

> Cook by **Indirect Heat Method** for charcoal, by **Indirect Heat Method (Low Heat)** for gas, for approximately 90 minutes or until juices run clear when thigh is pierced. See **Briquette Chart**, page 4, for extra coals. Baste frequently with Tandoori Basting Sauce.

Grilled Stuffed Tomatoes (page 73) and a rice pilaf would go well with this dish.   *Serves 4.*

Tandoori Basting Sauce

¼ cup melted butter
½ teaspoon nutmeg
½ teaspoon cinnamon
½ teaspoon coriander
2 tablespoons
   lemon juice

Combine all ingredients and blend well.

Chicken Monterey

Present this beautifully light creation, particularly appropriate for an elegant luncheon, on a bed of alfalfa sprouts or watercress.

2 whole chicken breasts
¼ cup olive oil
½ cup dry white wine
2 cloves garlic, crushed
½ teaspoon salt

2 ripe avocados
   Lemon juice
2 hard-boiled
   eggs, shelled

Remove the skin from each breast in 1 piece; set aside. Bone each breast in 1 piece and flatten to an even thickness. Combine the olive oil, wine, garlic and salt in a shallow bowl with boned chicken. Marinate 30 minutes at room temperature.

Halve the avocados lengthwise, pit and peel. Bathe in lemon juice. Put each avocado back together around an egg. Drain the breasts, reserving the marinade, and pat dry; wrap each around an avocado and wrap with skin to form 2 neat packages; sew or skewer skin.

> Grill by **Direct Heat Method** for charcoal, by **Indirect Heat Method (High Heat)** for gas, for about 30 minutes or until the meat is firm and springy. Turn the breasts frequently, basting with reserved marinade.

Let chicken stand 10 minutes before cutting in halves lengthwise. Drizzle with Tan Tara Honey Dressing (below).   *Serves 4.*

Tan Tara Honey Dressing

⅔ cup mayonnaise
¼ cup vegetable oil
2 tablespoons honey
1 tablespoon Dijon mustard
⅓ cup minced onion
1 teaspoon minced parsley
   Juice of ½ lemon

Combine all ingredients and blend well.
Makes about 1 cup.

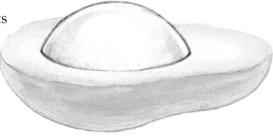

Sweet-and-Sour Chicken

Once again, coal cooking brings a special enhancement to a great favorite: Sweet-and-Sour Chicken. It's all done in the kettle.

1 broiler-fryer chicken
  (3 pounds)
½ cup soy sauce
1 cup pineapple juice
½ cup chicken stock
2 cloves garlic, minced
1 tablespoon grated gingerroot
¼ cup brown sugar, packed
¼ cup cider vinegar
1 green pepper, cut into
  1-inch squares
1 tomato, peeled, seeded,
  cut into 1-inch chunks
1 cup pineapple chunks
1 bunch scallions, sliced
  diagonally into 1-inch
  pieces
2 tablespoons cornstarch
¼ cup cold water

Wash and dry the chicken. Disjoint and chop into 2-inch pieces with a heavy cleaver. Combine the soy sauce, pineapple juice, stock, garlic, gingerroot, brown sugar and vinegar. Marinate the chicken in this mixture for 2 hours in the refrigerator.

Remove the chicken pieces from the marinade; set both aside. Then, line a baking pan (large and deep enough to hold the chicken and marinade) with foil; place the pepper, tomato, pineapple chunks and scallions on the bottom; pour the marinade over.

Grill by **Indirect Heat Method** for charcoal, by **Indirect Heat Method (Low Heat)** for gas. Brown the chicken pieces over the coals on either side of the grill for about 15 minutes. Transfer to pan with marinade and vegetables. Cook for 30 minutes.

To finish the sauce, remove the chicken pieces to a warm platter. Mix the cornstarch and water and add to the pan juices on grill; stir until thickened. Pour the sauce over the chicken and accompany with rice.   *Serves 4.*

Sesame Chicken

A Korean specialty, born over hot coals and savory with sesame oil.

2 pounds chicken thighs
¼ cup minced scallion
1 clove garlic, minced
1 teaspoon grated gingerroot
2 tablespoons sesame seed
1½ teaspoons sesame oil
¼ teaspoon cayenne pepper

Wash chicken thighs and pat dry. Combine well with remaining ingredients. Refrigerate for 2 hours.

> Grill by **Direct Heat Method** for charcoal, by **Indirect Heat Method (High Heat)** for gas, for 25 minutes or until nicely browned and cooked through.

Add Sweet-and-Sour Vegetables Skewers, (page 78) for an exotic meal. *Serves 4.*

Spiedini

Another gift from the Italian grill, basted and browned to a golden turn.

2 whole chicken breasts
   Paprika
1 pound sweet Italian sausage
6 large whole chicken livers
6 slices bacon
12 sage leaves or dried sage
12 large mushroom caps
6 tablespoons melted butter

Skin and bone the chicken breasts. Cut into 2-inch chunks and sprinkle lightly with paprika. Cut the sausage into 12 equal pieces. Cut chicken livers and bacon slices in half. Wrap each liver with bacon, tucking in 1 sage leaf or a pinch of dried sage. Thread all ingredients on skewers. Brush with melted butter.

> Grill by **Direct Heat Method** for charcoal, by **Indirect Heat Method (High Heat)** for gas. See page 7 for **Special Kebab Instructions.** Cook for about 25 minutes or until sausage is cooked and bacon browned. Turn and baste frequently with butter.

Present skewers on a bed of buttered noodles. *Serves 6.*

Turkey Talk

Sharpen up your knife, buy a whole turkey and separate it into two glorious feasts. Your family and friends will gobble it up. And that's a fact.

Barbecued Turkey

1 turkey (8 to 10 pounds) or
   4 to 5 pounds turkey parts
   Peanut oil
   Salt and freshly ground pepper

Disjoint the turkey, just as you would a chicken. Set the breast aside for another meal. Separate the wing joints (save the tips for stock). Using a heavy cleaver (or a friendly butcher), chop the legs, thighs and back into 2- to 2½-inch lengths. Make the pieces as equal in size and general bulk as possible for even cooking. Rub with oil and season with salt and pepper.

Honey-Soy Barbecue Sauce (page 59)

Grill by **Direct Heat Method** for charcoal, by **Indirect Heat Method (High Heat)** for gas, for 25 to 30 minutes or until nicely browned; test for doneness by cutting along the bone to be sure no pinkness remains. Baste with Honey-Soy Barbecue Sauce during the last 10 or 15 minutes of cooking.

Serves 6 to 8.

Buttered Breast of Turkey

Reserved turkey breast
or 1 whole turkey breast
(4 to 5 pounds)
½ cup butter, softened
Salt and freshly ground pepper
Peanut oil

Bone the turkey breast just as you would a whole chicken breast (Card **10b**). Remove the skin and set aside. Lay the breast, cut side up, on a board and flatten to an even thickness with a mallet. Spread the butter evenly over the meat and sprinkle with salt and pepper. Roll the meat tightly and wrap the skin around the cylindrical roast. Tie with cord every 2 inches. Rub the outside of the roast with butter.

> Roast by **Indirect Heat Method** for charcoal, by **Indirect Heat Method (Low Heat)** for gas, for 1 to 1½ hours or until a meat thermometer inserted in the center registers 170°. Baste frequently with peanut oil. See **Briquette Chart**, page 4, for extra coals.

Remove the roast and allow it to stand for 10 or 15 minutes before carving.   *Serves 6 to 8.*

Stuffed Buttered Breast: Use chopped apple and cooked pork sausages or sausage meat or use your favorite poultry stuffing. Roll as desired (see below). Tie and rub with butter. For self-basting, lay slices of bacon over the top of the roll.

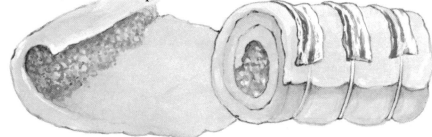

Peking Duck

The ultimate in barbecued duck, and China's most celebrated banquet dish.

1 duck (4 to 5 pounds), preferably wet-plucked with head and neck intact

Remove as much fat as possible from duck. Rinse the bird inside and out and pat dry. Now, believe it or not, the skin of the duck must be inflated so that it will dry thoroughly. Tie off the neck tightly with heavy twine. Sew up the bottom cavity opening tightly, folding over the skin edges, to form an airtight seal. If you are working with a supermarket duck, seal both the top and bottom cavities with your best surgical stitch.

Cut a small slit in the side of the neck, just large enough to insert the end of a straw. Insert the straw and blow air between the skin and flesh until the entire bird is inflated. Sew the slit tightly.

With twine or wire, fashion a hanging loop around the wings, legs or tail and suspend the duck over a basin in a *cool,* airy place to dry overnight. If this is not possible, position an electric fan to blow on the duck for 1 hour.

½ cup honey
1 cup water

Bring 2 quarts of water to a boil; immerse the duck or pour the water over the duck to scald the skin. It should turn almost white. Drain well and dry with paper towels. Combine the honey and 1 cup water and heat to boiling. Rub the honey water over the skin, saturating it completely. Hang the duck once more in a *cool,* airy place. The drying process will take 8 to 10 hours. (If an electric fan is used, drying will take 2 to 3 hours.) Take care that the duck is in a COOL place—the refrigerator if necessary—to prevent spoilage.

¼ cup sesame oil

Cook by **Indirect Heat Method** for charcoal, by **Indirect Heat Method (Low Heat)** for gas, for about 1½ hours or until the duck meat is done (the leg will move easily when rotated) and the skin is crispy and a deep golden brown. Baste with oil every 15 minutes. See **Briquette Chart,** page 4, for extra coals.

To serve, cut the skin, while still on the duck, into bite-sized diamond or rectangular shapes. Remove the skin or leave it on the bird as you prefer. Accompany with scallions, cut diagonally into 1-inch pieces, Duck Sauce (page 57) or Hoisin Sauce (page 57) and Steamed Buns (see below). To eat, peel off a round of steamed bun, place a piece of skin and a scallion strip on the bun, fold it over, dip it in the sauce and eat. Although the Chinese prepare the duck for the crisp, golden skin (and serve the meat in another dish at a subsequent meal), we devour the tender meat right along with the skin. *Serves 4.*

Steamed Buns

2 packages fan tan refrigerator rolls

Divide each roll in the center and place each half on a buttered or oiled square of aluminum foil. Place side by side in a steamer. Cover and steam over simmering water for about 10 minutes or until translucent and firm and no longer sticky. Separate the layers to eat.

Seafood

Paella Valenciana

Paella Valenciana combines an abundance of seafood with chicken, pork, vegetables and saffron rice. This exquisite meal requires little more than a chilled bottle of dry white wine to complete it. Guacamole, served in avocado shells, is a fine first course.

2 frozen lobster tails, thawed
½ pound medium shrimp
4 tablespoons olive oil
¼ pound scallops
¼ pound lean pork
1 large green pepper, chopped
1 large onion, chopped
2 cloves garlic, minced
1½ cups uncooked rice
3 cups chicken stock
2 large tomatoes, peeled, seeded and chopped
¼ teaspoon powdered saffron
2 teaspoons salt
¼ teaspoon pepper

1 chicken (2 to 2½ pounds), disjointed and cut into 2-inch pieces
2 tablespoons olive oil
1 package (10 ounces) frozen peas
6 cherrystone clams
6 mussels

Cut lobster tails (with shells) into 2-inch cubes. Remove legs from shrimp. Heat 2 tablespoons of the olive oil in a skillet and sauté the lobster, shrimp and scallops for 3 to 4 minutes. Set aside. Sauté the pork, green pepper, onion and garlic in the remaining 2 tablespoons olive oil until onions are translucent. Place the pork-vegetable mixture in a 4- to 5-quart casserole or a large foil pan. Stir in the rice, stock, tomatoes, saffron, salt and pepper. Set aside.

Brown the chicken at either side of the grill directly over the coals, for 10 to 15 minutes, basting with oil. Stir into casserole and cover. Cook by **Indirect Heat Method** for charcoal, by **Indirect Heat Method (Low Heat)** for gas, for 30 minutes. Stir occasionally, adding more stock if necessary. Stir in the reserved seafood and frozen peas. Arrange clams and mussels on top. Leave the casserole cover off and cook for 15 minutes or until clams and mussels open their shells.

Serve piping hot, directly from the casserole. *Serves 6.*

Stuffed Trout

This preparation was secured from the chef of one of the world's most elegant French restaurants. It is a true salute to the regal trout.

Fish Stuffing (below)
4 trout
1 tablespoon butter, softened
1 carrot, cut in ¼-inch dice
1 onion, cut in ¼-inch dice
Pinch of thyme
1 cup bottled clam juice
½ cup medium dry white wine

Prepare Stuffing and chill. Stuff trout and sew cavities closed. Generously butter the bottom of an aluminum foil pan large enough to hold the fish side by side. Spread the carrot and onion in the pan; sprinkle with thyme. Place the pan on the grill. Lay the fish on the vegetable bed; pour in the clam juice and wine. Cover the pan loosely with buttered aluminum foil.

> Cook by **Indirect Heat Method** for charcoal, by **Indirect Heat Method (Low Heat)** for gas, for 20 to 30 minutes or until the flesh along the backbone flakes easily.

½ cup light cream
4 tablespoons flour
4 tablespoons butter, softened
1 tablespoon lemon juice

Carefully remove the fish to a hot platter. Pour the pan juices with vegetables into a saucepan. Add the cream. Blend flour with butter and, over heat, gradually stir into sauce. Cook, stirring constantly, until thickened. Add lemon juice; correct seasonings. Serve this sauce on the side.   *Serves 4.*

Fish Stuffing

2 small carrots, finely chopped
2 tablespoons butter
4 medium mushrooms, minced
¼ cup minced celery heart
4 tablespoons flour
½ cup milk
4 egg yolks

Place the finely chopped carrots in a small saucepan and cover with boiling water. Simmer for 10 minutes; drain. Add the butter, mushrooms and celery and cook over low heat, stirring occasionally, for 10 minutes. Stir in the flour and cook, stirring, for 2 or 3 minutes. Remove from heat. Combine the milk and egg yolks; whip with a fork to blend and stir into the vegetable mixture. Heat and stir until mixture thickens. Cool and chill.

Grilled Whole Fish

A dish straight from Tokyo. In the variation, the method of preparation remains the same, but the seasonings become those of the Mediterranean.

1 whole fish (2 pounds)
2 scallions, minced
2 slices gingerroot, minced
½ teaspoon sugar
½ teaspoon salt
1 tablespoon soy sauce
1 tablespoon sake or dry sherry
1 tablespoon peanut oil or sesame oil

Peanut oil

Have the fish cleaned and scaled. Remove the fins but leave the head and tail intact. Score the fish on both sides—to the bone but not through it—with 2 or 3 parallel diagonal slashes. This allows heat and seasonings to penetrate and prevents curling. Combine the scallions, gingerroot, sugar, salt, soy, sake and oil. Rub the fish inside and out with this mixture. Allow to stand 30 minutes. Oil the grill and heat it over the coals. This will help prevent the fish from sticking.

Grill by **Direct Heat Method** for charcoal, by **Indirect Heat Method (High Heat)** for gas, for approximately 5 minutes per side, basting frequently with peanut oil. When the first side is nicely browned, turn and place fish on a fresh spot on the grill.

Serves 2 to 4.

Italian Variation

1 clove garlic, minced
5 sprigs rosemary, minced
3 tablespoons parsley, minced
1½ teaspoons salt
Freshly ground pepper
Few drops of olive oil

Combine ingredients and rub the scored fish with them. Grill as above, basting with a mixture of ¼ cup of olive oil and the juice of ½ lemon.

"Braised" Fish Fillets

From Germany, an easy, economical and highly practical way of preparing delicate fish fillets. Serve with a creamy dill sauce.

1 pound fish fillets
3 tablespoons butter
1 teaspoon salt
1 bay leaf
1 medium onion, thinly sliced
¼ cup dry white wine

Place a double layer of fish fillets in a large, buttered square of heavy-duty aluminum foil, sprinkle each layer with salt and dot with remaining butter. Add the bay leaf and sliced onion. Pour the wine over. Seal tightly.

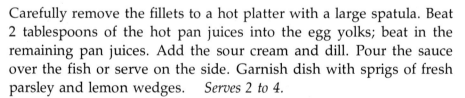

Cook by **Direct Heat Method** for charcoal, by **Indirect Heat Method (High Heat)** for gas, for about 10 minutes or until fish flakes easily when tested with a fork. Turn the packet over after 5 minutes.

2 egg yolks, beaten
½ cup sour cream
2 tablespoons fresh dill, chopped, or 1½ teaspoons dried dill weed

Carefully remove the fillets to a hot platter with a large spatula. Beat 2 tablespoons of the hot pan juices into the egg yolks; beat in the remaining pan juices. Add the sour cream and dill. Pour the sauce over the fish or serve on the side. Garnish dish with sprigs of fresh parsley and lemon wedges.   *Serves 2 to 4.*

Sweet-and-Sour Fish

If you buy 1-pound blocks of frozen fillets and thaw them in the package, they usually adhere in a block, making it easy to cut into uniform squares.

3 pounds halibut or haddock
  fillets
1 cup peanut oil
  Juice of 2 limes
3 tablespoons soy sauce
½ to 1 pound shrimp

If frozen, thaw fish slowly in the refrigerator. Cut fillets or thawed blocks into 1-inch cubes. Combine the oil, lime juice and soy sauce and pour over the fillets. Skewer the cubes, alternating with an occasional peeled, deveined shrimp. Reserve marinade for basting.

Grill by **Direct Heat Method** for charcoal, by **Indirect Heat Method (High Heat)** for gas, for about 10 minutes or until fish is opaque and flakes easily. See page 7 for **Special Kebab Instructions.** Turn only when necessary; then carefully. Baste sparingly.

Serve with Sweet-and-Sour Vegetable Skewers (page 78), Sweet-and-Sour Sauce (page 56) and steamed rice. *Serves 6 to 8.*

Curry Variation: Skewer the fish cubes with cucumber and scallion pieces and baste with oil while cooking. Serve with Curry Sauce (page 58) and bowls of toasted slivered almonds, raisins, chutney, peanuts and toasted coconut.

Mixed Seafood Grill

Variety spices up a celebration. Team this sampling of the sea's finest with a variety of excellent sauces. A salad bar selection of raw vegetables can also be dipped in the sauces for crunchy good appetizers.

- 2 **frozen lobster tails, thawed**
- 8 **medium shrimp**
- 12 **bay scallops**
- ½ **pound halibut**
- 8 **oysters, shucked**
- 12 **medium mushroom caps**
- ½ **cup melted butter**

Shell the lobster and cut it into 12 chunks. Shell and devein the shrimp. Dry the scallops. Cut the halibut into chunks, approximately the same size as the lobster chunks. Wipe the mushrooms clean with a damp cloth. Alternate the ingredients on skewers and brush with melted butter.

Grill by **Direct Heat Method** for charcoal, by **Indirect Heat Method (High Heat)** for gas, for 6 to 8 minutes or until seafood is opaque and cooked through. See page 7 for **Special Kebab Instructions.** Don't pack the skewers tightly; leave room for the heat to circulate. Turn once; baste with butter.

Serve with Lemon Butter (below), Mustard Mayonnaise (page 54) and Artichoke Hearts (page 74). Add a whopping big mixed green salad. Other sauces you might offer include Béarnaise Sauce (page 53), Curry Sauce (page 58), Tartar Sauce (page 54) and Cocktail Sauce (page 55).   *Serves 4 to 6.*

Lemon Butter

- ¼ **pound butter**
- **Juice of 1 lemon**

Melt the butter in a pan over the coals. Do not let it bubble or boil. Stir in the lemon juice with a fork or whisk.   *Makes about ½ cup.*

Split Roast Lobster

The only thing I can imagine that's more delightful than Split Roast Lobster with Tomalley Butter is two Split Roast Lobsters with Tomalley Butter.

1 lobster (1½ to 2 pounds) per serving
Melted butter

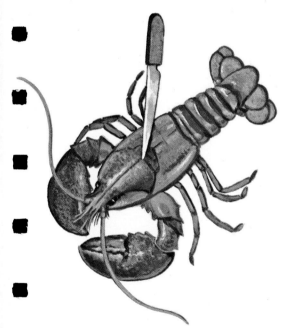

Have the lobster split and cleaned, reserving the tomalley and coral, as close to cooking time as possible. Or, do it yourself just before cooking. Place a live lobster, legs down, on a cutting board and hold it in place with a towel over the head and claws. To sever the spinal cord, plunge the point of a heavy, sharp knife into the back where the chest and tail meet. Turn the lobster over and split it lengthwise from head to tail. Remove the stomach (small sack inside the head) and dark intestinal vein running through the body and discard. Remove the tomalley (the gray matter inside the chest) and the coral (reddish eggs found in female lobsters); reserve for Tomalley Butter. Brush the cut side of the lobster generously with butter and place on the grill, cut side up.

> Grill by **Direct Heat Method** for charcoal, by **Indirect Heat Method (High Heat)** for gas, for 15 to 20 minutes or until cooked through (flesh appears opaque). Baste frequently with melted butter.

Serve with Tomalley Butter (below) and garnish with lemon wedges. *Serves 1.*

Tomalley Butter

Mash the tomalley and coral of each lobster with 1 tablespoon cognac. Blend in ½ cup softened butter, ½ teaspoon tarragon and freshly ground pepper to taste.

Sauces

Béarnaise Sauce

Sauces are often the magic touch that turns plain food into elegant fare. Present Beef Kebabs with an array of sauces and call it "fondue."

1 tablespoon minced shallot
   or scallion
½ teaspoon tarragon
2 tablespoons wine vinegar
3 egg yolks
1 teaspoon Dijon mustard
1 tablespoon lemon juice
½ pound butter

Simmer shallot, tarragon and vinegar in a saucepan, stirring constantly, until liquid evaporates. Combine the shallot-tarragon mixture with the egg yolks, mustard and lemon juice in a blender jar. Turn the blender quickly on and off at high speed several times to blend the ingredients. Melt the butter to bubbling. Turn the blender on high speed and immediately begin to pour the butter in a slow but steady stream. As soon as the butter is mixed in, turn the blender off. Serve with beef or fish.   *Makes about 1 cup.*

Hollandaise Sauce

3 egg yolks
2 teaspoons lemon juice
½ teaspoon salt
   Dash of cayenne pepper
¼ pound sweet butter

Combine the yolks, lemon juice, salt and cayenne in a blender jar. Turn the blender on, then quickly off to blend ingredients. Heat the butter in a pan until bubbly. Turn the blender on high. Pour in the hot butter in a slow but steady stream. As soon as the butter is mixed in, turn the blender off.

To make this sauce in a double boiler, melt the butter over gently simmering water. Stir the yolks, lemon juice, salt and cayenne together to blend; beat into the melted butter and stir constantly until thickened. If the sauce curdles, beat in a tablespoon or 2 of hot water.

Serve with asparagus or broccoli, fish or chicken.   *Makes 1 cup.*

Aïoli

4 cloves garlic
2 egg yolks
1 cup olive oil
1 teaspoon lemon juice
¾ teaspoon salt
¼ teaspoon pepper

Trim, crush and peel the garlic; pulverize. Add the egg yolks and mix thoroughly. Using a wire whisk, beat in the olive oil, drop by drop, until the sauce is the consistency of mayonnaise. Stir in the lemon juice, salt and pepper. Serve with fish, cold meats or with raw vegetables as a dip. *Makes about 1¼ cups.*

Tartar Sauce

1 cup mayonnaise
¼ cup chopped parsley
¼ cup chopped chives
1 teaspoon sweet pickle relish
1 teaspoon sweet pickle
   relish juice

Combine ingredients and puree in a blender. Serve with fish. *Makes about 1½ cups.*

Mustard Mayonnaise

1 cup mayonnaise
2 tablespoons Dijon mustard
2 tablespoons dry white wine

Combine all ingredients; blend until smooth. Serve with cold meats, poultry or artichokes. *Makes about 1 cup.*

Roquefort Sauce

¼ cup butter, softened
¼ pound Roquefort cheese
1 clove garlic, pressed
1 tablespoon minced scallion
1 tablespoon cognac or brandy

Combine all ingredients; cream to blend. Serve with beef or with raw vegetables as a dip. *Makes ¾ cup.*

Cocktail Sauce

¾ cup catsup
⅓ cup lemon juice
¼ cup minced celery
1½ tablespoons prepared horseradish
½ teaspoon grated onion
Salt and Tabasco sauce to taste

Combine ingredients and blend well. Serve with shellfish. *Makes about 1¼ cups.*

Sweet-and-Sour Sauce

1¾ cups water or chicken stock
1 cup brown sugar, packed, or honey
1 cup cider vinegar
   Juice of 1 lemon
2 scallions, minced
¼ cup catsup
2 tablespoons dry sherry
2 tablespoons soy sauce
2 tablespoons cornstarch
¼ cup cold water

Combine water, brown sugar, vinegar, lemon juice, scallions, catsup, sherry and soy sauce in a saucepan. Bring to a boil. Combine cornstarch with water. Add to sauce and stir until liquid clears and thickens. Serve hot. Store covered in refrigerator. Serve with poultry, pork, fish or vegetables. *Makes about 4 cups.*

Hoisin Sauce I

1 cup hoisin sauce
½ cup sugar

Combine sauce with sugar and blend well. Serve with duck, chicken, beef or pork.   *Makes 1 cup.*

Hoisin Sauce II

1 cup hoisin sauce
½ cup soy sauce
1 teaspoon sesame oil

Combine ingredients and blend well. Serve with duck, chicken, beef or pork.   *Makes 1½ cups.*

Duck Sauce

1 cup apricot jam
1 pound plums, canned or fresh, peeled, pitted and finely chopped
⅛ teaspoon cayenne pepper
½ teaspoon salt
3 tablespoons water
3 to 4 tablespoons vinegar

Combine the ingredients in a heavy saucepan. Simmer 30 minutes, stirring occasionally. Cool and store covered in the refrigerator. The sauce will keep for several months. Serve with most Oriental poultry, beef, pork and shellfish dishes.   *Makes about 2 cups.*

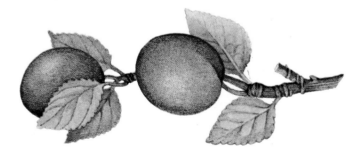

Curry Sauce

5 tablespoons butter
1 onion, minced
1 apple, peeled, cored and
  minced
1 stalk celery, minced
4 tablespoons flour
1 to 3 tablespoons curry power
3 cups chicken stock

Heat the butter in a saucepan and slightly brown the onion, apple and celery. Sprinkle with flour and curry powder; cook and stir a few minutes more. Add the stock, a little at a time to begin with, stirring to blend. Simmer 45 minutes.

¼ to ½ cup cream
  Salt, freshly ground pepper
  and lemon juice to taste
2 tablespoons chutney

Stir in the cream and season to taste with salt, pepper and lemon juice. Add the chutney just before serving. Surround the sauceboat with bowls of raisins, toasted slivered almonds, chutney and hot rice. *Makes about 3 cups.*

Yogurt Sauce

1 cup unflavored yogurt
1 cucumber, peeled, seeded, grated and drained
1 tomato, peeled, seeded, finely chopped and drained
1 tablespoon minced onion
1 small clove garlic, pressed or minced
1 tablespoon chopped parsley
¼ teaspoon dried mint leaves, crumbled
¼ teaspoon salt

Stir yogurt until smooth. Combine with remaining ingredients. Chill 1 hour. Serve with lamb. *Makes about 2 cups.*

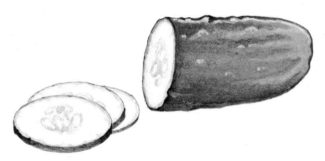

Honey-Soy Barbecue Sauce

½ cup soy sauce
¾ cup catsup
¾ cup honey
3 cloves garlic, pressed
½ teaspoon Tabasco sauce (less if desired)

Combine ingredients and blend well. Serve with beef, pork, chicken or fish. *Makes 2 cups.*

Smoky Barbecue Sauce

2 tablespoons butter
2 cloves garlic, pressed
½ cup finely chopped onion
½ cup finely chopped green pepper
½ cup finely chopped celery
½ teaspoon oregano
½ teaspoon basil
½ teaspoon cinnamon
1 teaspoon salt
  Juice of 1 lemon (reserve reamed shell)
⅛ teaspoon Tabasco sauce
1½ tablespoons Worcestershire sauce
1½ tablespoons "liquid smoke"
2 cups catsup
1 cup water
½ cup cider vinegar

Heat the butter in a 2-quart saucepan; add the garlic, onion, green pepper and celery and cook over medium heat for about 5 minutes, stirring frequently. Add seasonings and cook several minutes more. Add lemon juice and reamed shell and remaining ingredients. Simmer 30 minutes, stirring occasionally. Serve with beef, pork, chicken or fish. *Makes about 5 cups.*

Korean Marinade

3 tablespoons vegetable oil
1 tablespoon sesame oil
½ cup soy sauce
1 tablespoon vinegar
2 cloves garlic, pressed or
   minced
   Cayenne pepper to taste
2 tablespoons toasted sesame
   seed, crushed

Combine all ingredients and blend well. Use with chicken, pork or fish. *Makes about 1¼ cups.*

Teriyaki Marinade

1 cup soy sauce
½ cup sake or dry vermouth
½ cup sugar
1 tablespoon tomato paste
   (optional)
2 cloves garlic, pressed or
   minced
1 teaspoon grated gingerroot

Combine all ingredients and blend well. Use with chicken, pork or fish.
Makes about 2 cups.

Wok
Cooking

Beef with Snow Peas

1 pound beef sirloin
2 teaspoons cornstarch
2 teaspoons soy sauce
2 cloves garlic
1 medium onion

7 tablespoons peanut oil
3 tablespoons canned
  bean sauce
1 package frozen Chinese
  snow peas, thawed

Whether it be meat, seafood or vegetables, you can be sure that any food cooked in a wok will be delicious and extra nutritious. Rice is the perfect go-with for Oriental dishes.

Cut the beef into 2½x1x⅛-inch strips. Combine the cornstarch and soy sauce and stir into the beef strips. Cut the onion lengthwise into quarters; then cut the strips crosswise into ¼-inch slices. Crush and peel the garlic.

Cook by the **Wok Method.** See page 7 for both charcoal and gas. Pour 4 tablespoons of the oil into the hot wok and stir-fry the crushed garlic until it is browned; remove and discard. Add the beef mixture and stir-fry just until it loses its redness; remove to a warm dish and set aside. Pour the remaining 3 tablespoons oil into the wok and stir-fry the onion for 2 minutes. Add the bean sauce. Cook and stir for a few minutes more or until the onion is tender. Add the snow peas. Stir-fry for a few minutes, until the snow peas are tender-crisp. Add the beef mixture and stir until heated through.

Serve immediately. *Serves 2 American style, 4 Chinese style.*

Asparagus Variation: Break off the tough ends of 2 pounds of asparagus and cut the stalks on the diagonal into 1½-inch lengths. Add to the wok in place of the snow peas following the above recipe; stir-fry for a few minutes; cover and cook until the asparagus is tender-crisp and bright green. Add beef mixture and stir until heated through.

Szechwan Shrimp

Here's a great recipe, poetically called "Golden Hooks," from the Szechwan school of cooking. The shell holds the flavorful marinade next to the flesh.

1 pound medium shrimp
6 tablespoons soy sauce
¼ cup dry sherry
½ teaspoon sesame oil
2 scallions, chopped
2 chunks (1 inch each)
   gingerroot, crushed
½ teaspoon salt
1 teaspoon sugar
1 dried hot red pepper,
   seeded and crushed

1 tablespoon peanut oil

Clean the shrimp without removing the shells: Pull off the legs and slit the shell down the back; carefully lift out the black vein without loosening the shell. Rinse the shrimp quickly. Combine the remaining ingredients except peanut oil. Add the shrimp and stir. Refrigerate for 2 to 3 hours, stirring occasionally. Remove shrimp from marinade and dry thoroughly. Reserve marinade.

Cook by the **Wok Method.** See page 7 for both charcoal and gas. Add the oil to the hot wok; stir to coat bottom. Add the shrimp and stir-fry for 3 to 4 minutes. DO NOT OVERCOOK. Shrimp are done when they turn pink. Pour in the reserved marinade and bring to a boil.

Serve immediately.   *Serves 2 as a main dish, 4 as an appetizer.*

Bacon and Cabbage

This savory Old World blend of cabbage, bacon and onion is prepared quickly and easily in a wok. Don't neglect the variations.

½ pound sliced bacon
1 onion
1 small head cabbage

Salt

Cut the bacon crosswise into ½-inch pieces. Chop the onion and cut the cabbage into 1½-inch chunks.

Cook by the **Wok Method.** See page 7 for both charcoal and gas. Cook and stir bacon in the wok until lightly browned. Then add onion and continue stir-frying until onion is tender and translucent. Spoon out half the bacon fat. Add cabbage and toss to mix ingredients. Add salt to taste. Continue stir-frying until cabbage is just tender-crisp.

The flavor of this dish brings out the best in a roast duck, grilled sausages or a juicy pork roast. *Serves 6.*

Sweet-and-Sour Bacon and Cabbage: Pour Sweet-and-Sour Sauce (page 56) over the finished cabbage.

Creamed Bacon and Cabbage: Whip 1 cup sour cream into the finished dish. Heat through. (Do not boil.)

Hors d'Oeuvres

Don't forget to start your meal with some tasty cook-on-the-grill hors d'oeuvres. No need to limit your cookout expertise to the main course—show off your skills over cocktails with the intriguing appetizers found on the following pages. At an outdoor party, your Weber Kettle will become the focal point of the gathering, with guests doing their own cooking and, of course, advising the chef.

Hors d'oeuvre possibilities are scattered throughout the book. In many cases, all you need do is adjust the amount of ingredients indicated for a main dish, depending on the number of guests you are serving. Pineapple Pork Kebabs and Beef Skewers are perfect examples. You can simply quarter the large Pitas, and you'll have Turkish Tacos for hors d'oeuvres. And don't overlook the sausages. These suggestions add up to one thing—a terrific party!

Roasted Olives

These tasty tidbits are real appetite teasers. They'll vanish in a hurry.

12 slices bacon
24 large green olives, pitted

Cut the bacon in half crosswise and broil until partially cooked but still flexible. Wrap the olives in bacon and skewer through the loose bacon ends to secure.

> Grill by **Direct Heat Method** for charcoal, by **Indirect Heat Method (High Heat)** for gas, for about 15 minutes or until bacon is crisp and browned.

Makes 24 appetizers.

Rumaki

We all know these are great from the broiler, but just try them from the grill!

1 pound chicken livers
1 can (5 ounces) water chestnuts
10 to 12 ounces sliced bacon

Rinse and drain the livers; cut in half. Rinse and drain the water chestnuts; slice into ¼-inch rounds. Cut the bacon in half crosswise; fry until partially cooked. Wrap each piece of liver and 1 or 2 chestnut rounds with a half slice of bacon. Secure with a wooden pick.

> Grill by **Direct Heat Method** for charcoal, by **Indirect Heat Method (High Heat)** for gas. See page 7 for **Special Kebab Instructions.** Cook for 10 to 15 minutes or until bacon is crispy.

Makes 30 to 36 appetizers.

Chicken Wings

An adaptation of a delicious Chinese recipe, browned to crispy succulence.

8 to 10 chicken wings
½ cup chicken stock
¼ cup soy sauce
¼ cup dry sherry
2 scallions
2 tablespoons brown sugar

Disjoint the wings, discarding the tips. Place the wings with the remaining ingredients in a foil pan.

> Cook by **Indirect Heat Method** for charcoal, by **Indirect Heat Method (Low Heat)** for gas, for 30 minutes. Brown the wings at either side of the grill directly over hot coals for 10 to 15 minutes (cover off). Keep the sauce hot.

Serve the wings on a warmed platter with the cooking liquid (scallions removed) as a dipping sauce. *Makes 16 to 20 appetizers.*

Mushroom and Scallop Skewers

12 bay scallops
12 mushroom caps
½ cup melted butter
Juice of 1 lemon
Salt and freshly ground pepper

Bay scallops are suggested, but they are more expensive and less available than deep-sea scallops. If you use the latter, cut in half before skewering.

Clean and dry the scallops and mushroom caps. Nestle a scallop in each mushroom cap, skewer through the side of the mushroom, taking care to pierce the scallop to hold it in place. Brush generously with melted butter and sprinkle with lemon juice, salt and pepper.

> Grill by **Direct Heat Method** for charcoal, by **Indirect Heat Method (High Heat)** for gas, for 7 to 10 minutes or until scallops are springy-firm and opaque. Turn and baste frequently with melted butter.

Serve with lemon wedges and remaining butter.   *Makes 12 appetizers.*

Mushroom and Scallop Teriyaki

½ cup soy sauce
¼ cup sugar
2 tablespoons peanut oil
1 tablespoon dry sherry
1 teaspoon grated gingerroot
1 clove garlic, crushed

Combine ingredients and blend well. Skewer as above. Brush generously with sauce and grill as above, except baste with sauce instead of butter.

Oysters à la Bourguignonne

A delicious and elegant first course. The same recipe can be used for clams.

**12 oysters on the half shell
Rock salt**

Select 4 aluminum foil pans large enough to hold 3 oysters each. Arrange a bed of rock salt in each. Dampen the salt and place pans on the grill to heat.

**½ cup fine bread crumbs
3 tablespoons butter
3 slices bacon**

Combine the bread crumbs with the butter in a skillet; stir over medium heat until browned. Reserve. Partially cook the bacon until lightly browned but still flexible. Reserve.

**½ cup butter, softened
1 teaspoon finely chopped shallot
1 small clove garlic, chopped
1 tablespoon chopped parsley
½ teaspoon tarragon
Salt and freshly ground pepper**

Cream together the butter, shallot, garlic, parsley, tarragon, salt and pepper and spread a scant tablespoon on each oyster. Sprinkle each with reserved browned crumbs. Cut the reserved precooked bacon into 12 pieces and top each oyster with a bacon piece. Place 3 oysters in each pan, pressing the shells down into the rock salt to stabilize them.

> Cook by **Direct Heat Method** for charcoal, by **Indirect Heat Method (High Heat)** for gas, for 7 to 10 minutes or until butter is bubbly and oysters are heated through.

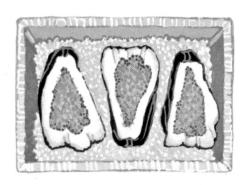

Serve immediately.   *Serves 12 as an appetizer or 4 as a first course.*

Luau Ribs

The best and moistest barbecued ribs I've ever tasted are made on the island of Molokai by a beautiful grandmother named Haa Haa. Here's the recipe.

6 **pounds spareribs**
1 **cup soy sauce**
½ **cup water**
¼ **cup dry sherry**
¼ **cup pineapple juice**
½ **cup brown sugar, firmly packed**
2 **cloves garlic, minced or pressed**
6 **thin slices gingerroot**

If preparing as an appetizer, have the butcher saw the ribs in half and divide into 2- or 3-rib sections. If preparing as a main course, separate the whole ribs into serving-size pieces. Simmer 30 minutes in salted water to cover. Drain. Combine remaining ingredients and pour over ribs. Refrigerate for 2 to 3 hours. Remove ribs from the marinade. Pour marinade into a small saucepan and heat.

Grill ribs by **Indirect Heat Method** for charcoal, by **Indirect Heat Method (Low Heat)** for gas, for about 45 minutes. Baste with marinade.

Serves 12 as an appetizer, 6 as a main course.

Roast Mushrooms

Here is a very gentle way to enhance the delicate flavor of the mushroom.

1 **pound mushrooms**
2 **tablespoons melted butter or olive oil**
1 **clove garlic, pressed**
2 **tablespoons dry white wine**
  Dash of Worcestershire sauce
  Salt and freshly ground pepper

Remove the mushroom stems. Wipe the caps clean with a damp cloth. Combine with remaining ingredients in a square of heavy-duty aluminum foil. Seal tightly. Let stand 1 hour at room temperature.

Cook by **Indirect Heat Method** for charcoal, by **Indirect Heat Method (Low Heat)** for gas, for 20 to 25 minutes.

Good also as a side dish with beef, chicken or fish.   *Serves 4.*

Vegetables

Ratatouille

Ratatouille is so special that I often serve it as the main course!

1 medium eggplant, sliced
2 onions, thinly sliced
4 small zucchini, sliced
2 tomatoes, peeled, seeded and cut into wedges
2 green peppers, seeded and sliced into rings
2 cloves garlic, pressed
½ cup olive oil
1 tablespoon fresh basil or 1 teaspoon dried basil
Salt and freshly ground pepper

Use a large skillet, or cut 6 to 8 ample squares of heavy-duty aluminum foil, depending on the number of diners. Combine ingredients in skillet and cover, or divide the ingredients equally between the foil squares. Seal tightly.

> Grill by **Direct Heat Method** for charcoal, by **Indirect Heat Method (High Heat)** for gas, for about 1 hour. Check one of the packets after 30 minutes to be sure cooking is proceeding apace.

Serve hot or cold with beef, fish, chicken or lamb—it's even served with eggs. *Serves 6 to 8.*

Stuffed Tomatoes

Grilled tomatoes have always been a favorite because of their color value. Here's a better reason for serving them—their taste.

2 large, firm tomatoes
3 tablespoons dry bread crumbs
⅛ teaspoon garlic powder
Pinch of dried basil
2 tablespoons chopped parsley
¼ cup grated cheese (brick, Muenster, mozzarella or Swiss)
2 tablespoons butter, softened

Cut the tomatoes in half crosswise; scrape out the seeds with a teaspoon. Combine the remaining ingredients; pack the mixture into the tomato cavities.

> Grill cut side up by **Direct Heat Method** for charcoal, by **Indirect Heat Method (High Heat)** for gas, for about 10 minutes or until tomatoes are heated through and cheese is melted.

Serve with roasts or grilled meats, fish or poultry. *Serves 4.*

Artichoke Hearts

The creative genius of the Italian cook shines through in this savory side dish of Fondi di Carciofi—hearts of artichoke.

2 large artichokes
½ cup water
2 tablespoons lemon juice

Snap off the bottom leaves, then trim the bulb with a sharp knife to remove all tough leaf fibers. Trim the stem and top; quarter the bulb lengthwise and remove the choke. Combine water and 2 tablespoons lemon juice. Slice the artichoke lengthwise into thin wedges and rinse in the acidulated water.

Juice of ½ lemon
1 clove garlic, pressed
2 tablespoons dry white wine
2 tablespoons olive oil
Pinch of dried basil
Salt and freshly ground
pepper

Combine the remaining ingredients, and stir in the artichoke wedges, tossing to blend flavors and coat the pieces. Seal in heavy-duty aluminum foil.

Cook by **Indirect Heat Method** for charcoal, by **Indirect Heat Method (Low Heat)** for gas, for 30 minutes or until artichokes are tender.

These go well with Steak au Poivre (page 9), Beef Bird Casserole (page 14) or Stuffed Lamb (page 29).   *Serves 4.*

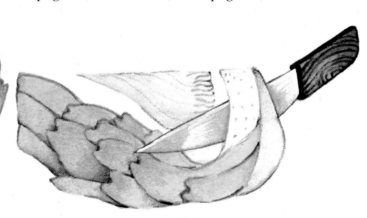

Betty's Beans

A hearty all-American barbecue bean dish.

½ pound bacon, chopped
½ cup finely chopped onion
½ cup finely chopped green
  pepper
½ cup brown sugar, firmly packed
1 can (6 ounces) tomato paste
2 tomato paste cans water
2 tablespoons Worcestershire
  sauce
2 cans (15 ounces each)
  large butter beans

Brown the bacon in a large frying pan. Pour off all but 2 to 3 table-spoons of the grease. Add onion, green pepper, brown sugar, tomato paste, water and Worcestershire. Simmer 30 minutes, stirring frequently. Drain the beans and combine with sauce in 1 or 2 aluminum foil baking pans.

> Cook by **Indirect Heat Method** for charcoal, by **Indirect Heat Method (Low Heat)** for gas, for 1 hour. Stir after 30 minutes.

This bean dish goes hand-in-hand with thick juicy burgers, grilled at either side of the kettle. *Serves 6.*

Grilled Eggplant

Excess moisture should be removed from eggplant. This is why the salted slices are left to stand for 30 minutes.

2 medium eggplants, cut in
  ½-inch slices
  Salt
½ cup olive oil
1 clove garlic, crushed

Sprinkle the eggplant with salt and allow to stand for 30 minutes. Combine the oil and garlic. Press the eggplant slices dry between paper towels. Brush with oil.

> Grill by **Direct Heat Method** for charcoal, by **Indirect Heat Method (High Heat)** for gas, for 3 to 4 minutes per side or until golden brown and soft. Baste with oil before turning.

Great with all grills and roasts, but especially lamb. *Serves 6.*

Baked Squash

This tender, delicious, remarkable squash dresses up any meal.

2 medium acorn squash
4 tablespoons butter
4 to 8 slices crisp-cooked bacon

Cut the squash in half crosswise and scoop out the seeds and fibers. Place a tablespoon of butter in the cavity of each and top with crumbled bacon. Seal individually in heavy-duty aluminum foil.

> Cook by **Indirect Heat Method** for charcoal, by **Indirect Heat Method (Low Heat)** for gas, for approximately 1 hour or until squash is soft clear through.

Goes well with any roast as a starch-vegetable.   *Serves 4.*

Banana-Stuffed Sweet Potatoes

A delicious Hawaiian treatment for the sweet potato, great for gala repasts.

3 hot baked sweet potatoes
3 tablespoons butter, softened
1 teaspoon grated orange rind
4 tablespoons orange juice
2 tablespoons dark rum
1 cup chopped pineapple, well drained
3 bananas, sliced
  Brown sugar
  Grated coconut

Cut the still-hot baked potatoes in half lengthwise and scoop out the flesh, leaving a ¼-inch shell. Mash the potato with the butter. Add the orange rind and juice, rum and pineapple. Mix thoroughly. Cut 3 ample squares of heavy-duty aluminum foil and place 2 shells on each. Line shell bottoms with banana slices and fill with sweet potato mixture. Top with banana slices, brown sugar and coconut.

> Cook by **Indirect Heat Method** for charcoal, by **Indirect Heat Method (Low Heat)** for gas, for 30 minutes.

A beautiful companion to roast pork, chicken or turkey.   *Serves 4.*

Sweet Glazed Carrots

This recipe of my mother's is responsible for unknown numbers of converts to the Cooked Carrot Fan Club of America. Try them on your carrot haters.

6 medium carrots
¼ cup butter

Slice the carrots into paper-thin rounds. Butter an ample sheet of heavy-duty aluminum foil. Place the carrot slices in the foil and dot with the remaining butter. Seal the packet.

> Cook by **Indirect Heat Method** for charcoal, by **Indirect Heat Method (Low Heat)** for gas, for 30 minutes or until carrots are tender. Stir in the confectioners' sugar.

**2 tablespoons confectioners'
    sugar**

Serves 4.

Grilled Peppers

Something very special happens to a pepper when it is roasted and peeled. The subtle dressing is exactly the right touch.

2 tablespoons olive oil
1 clove garlic, crushed

Combine the oil and crushed garlic and let stand for 1 hour.

> Grill by **Direct Heat Method** for charcoal, by **Indirect Heat Method (High Heat)** for gas, for about 10 minutes. Turn as skin blisters and blackens until entire pepper is done.

4 firm green peppers

Scrape and peel the hot skin away. (If serving cold, remove the skin under running water.) Cut the pepper into strips and discard the seeds. Remove the garlic from the oil and pour the oil over the pepper strips. Sprinkle with a dash of vinegar. Serve hot or cold with beef, fish or chicken. *Serves 4.*

Dash of vinegar

Sweet-and-Sour Vegetable Skewers

It's the fresh pineapple that gives this dish its extraordinary savor.

½ pineapple, peeled, cored
  and cut into 1-inch cubes
2 large green peppers, seeded
  and cut into 1-inch squares
16 cherry tomatoes
2 cucumbers, peeled, halved
  lengthwise and cut into
  ¼-inch slices
4 sweet pickles, cut into
  ¼-inch slices
6 to 8 scallions (white part
  only), cut diagonally into
  1-inch lengths
  Peanut oil

Alternate pineapple and vegetables on skewers; baste with oil.

Grill by **Direct Heat Method** for charcoal, by **Indirect Heat Method (High Heat)** for gas. See page 7 for **Special Kebab Instructions.** Cook for 15 to 20 minutes. Turn and baste frequently.

Serve with roast chicken, pork or beef or grilled fish. *Serves 6 to 8.*

Roast Potatoes

These potatoes are crispy, browned and flavorful with roast drippings.

4 medium baking potatoes,
  unpeeled
  Roast drippings
  or bacon fat

Cut potatoes into chunks. Skewer and brush with drippings.

Grill by **Indirect Heat Method** for charcoal, by **Indirect Heat Method (Low Heat)** for gas, for 30 minutes. For charcoal, move potatoes after 15 minutes to either side of the grill over coals for 10 to 15 minutes to brown. Turn and baste frequently with drippings.

Perfect accompanying a beef or pork roast. *Serves 4 to 6.*

Index

Page entries in **boldface** type refer to cards.

Page entries in **boldface** type refer to cards.

Roast Beef

Cooking Chart • Charcoal or Gas Kettles

TYPE OF ROAST	DONENESS	INTERNAL TEMP.*	APPROX. MIN. PER LB.
Rib roast (4-6 lbs.)	Rare Medium Well Done	140° 160° 170°	18-20 20-25 25-30
Rib roast (6-8 lbs.)	Rare Medium Well Done	140° 160° 170°	16-18 18-20 20-22
Rib eye (4-6 lbs.)	Rare Medium Well Done	140° 160° 170°	16-18 18-20 20-22
Tenderloin, whole (4-6 lbs.)		140°-160°	40-60 ready to serve
Tenderloin, half (2-3 lbs.)		140°-160°	40-60 ready to serve
Rump, rolled (4-6 lbs.)		150°-170°	18-22 ready to serve
Sirloin tip (3½-4 lbs.)		140°-170°	25-30 ready to serve
(6-8 lbs.)		140°-170°	20-25 ready to serve

Steaks

Cooking Chart • Charcoal or Gas Kettles

THICKNESS OF STEAK	RARE		MEDIUM		WELL DONE	
	1ST SIDE	2ND SIDE	1ST SIDE	2ND SIDE	1ST SIDE	2ND SIDE
1 inch	3 min.	3-4 min.	4 min.	4-5 min.	5 min.	6 min.
1½ inches	5 min.	6 min.	7 min.	8 min.	9 min.	10-11 min.
2 inches	7 min.	8 min.	9 min.	9-10 min.	10 min.	11-12 min.

Burgers

Cooking Chart
Charcoal or Gas Kettles

THICKNESS OF BURGER	APPROX. MINUTES PER SIDE		
	RARE	MEDIUM	WELL DONE
¾ inch	3	4	5
1 inch	4 to 5	5 to 6	6 to 7

Turkey

Cooking Chart
Charcoal or Gas Kettles

FRESH OR THAWED FROZEN READY-TO COOK WEIGHT (POUNDS)	INTERNAL TEMP.*	APPROX. COOKING TIME IN HOURS
Unstuffed 6-8 8-12 12-16 16-20	185° 185° 185° 185°	2 to 2¾ 2½ to 3¾ 3½ to 4 4½ to 5
Boneless turkey roll 2-5 5-10	175° 175°	1½ to 2 2 to 3½

For stuffed turkeys, allow about 3 to 5 minutes more per pound.

*If you plan to let the roast stand for 20 minutes (and this is recommended), reduce Internal Temperature reading by 5°-10°.

Roast Lamb

Cooking Chart • Charcoal or Gas Kettles

TYPE OF ROAST	DONENESS	INTERNAL TEMP.*	APPROX. MIN. PER LB.
Leg (5-9 lbs.)	Rare	140°	18-22
	Medium	160°	22-28
	Well Done	170°	28-33
Leg, shank half (3-4 lbs.)	Rare	140°	22-28
	Medium	160°	28-33
	Well Done	170°	33-38
Leg, sirloin half (3-4 lbs.)	Rare	140°	18-22
	Medium	160°	22-28
	Well Done	170°	28-33
Leg, boneless (4-7 lbs.)	Rare	140°	22-28
	Medium	160°	28-33
	Well Done	170°	33-38
Crown roast (2½-4 lbs.)	Rare	140°	28-33
	Medium	160°	33-38
	Well Done	170°	38-43
Shoulder, square cut (4-6 lbs.)	Medium	160°	22-28
	Well Done	170°	28-33
Shoulder, boneless	Rare	140°	28-33
	Medium	160°	33-38
	Well Done	170°	38-43
Rib (1½-2 lbs.)	Rare	140°	30-35
	Medium	160°	35-40
	Well Done	170°	40-45
Rib (2-3 lbs.)	Rare	140°	25-30
	Medium	160°	30-35
	Well Done	170°	35-40
Shoulder cushion (3½-5 lbs.)		170°	28-33 ready to serve

*If you plan to let the roast stand for 20 minutes (and this is recommended), reduce Internal Temperature reading by 10°.

Roast Pork

Cooking Chart • Charcoal or Gas Kettles

TYPE OF ROAST	INTERNAL TEMP.*	APPROX. MIN. PER LB.
Loin, center (3-5 lbs.)	170°	25-30
Loin, half (5-7 lbs.)	170°	30-35
Blade, or sirloin, (3-4 lbs.)	170°	35-40
Loin, top (double) (3-5 lbs.)	170°	25-40
Loin, top (4-6 lbs.)	170°	25-30
Crown (4-6 lbs.)	170°	25-30
Leg (fresh ham), (bone-in, 12-16 lbs.)	170°	18-24
Leg (fresh ham), (boneless, 5-8 lbs.)	170°	18-24
Half (5-8 lbs.)	170°	25-30
Tenderloin (½-1 lb.)	170°	45-60

*All pork should be cooked to 170° Internal Temperature, except fully cooked ham. However, if you plan to let the roast stand for 20 minutes (and this is recommended), the Internal Temperature should be 160°.

Foil Wrapped Vegetables
Cooking Chart
Charcoal or Gas Kettles

| VEGETABLE | MINUTES | |
	FRESH	FROZEN
Artichoke Hearts	—	20-25
Asparagus Whole or 2-inch pieces	10-20	10-20
Beans: Green, Italian, wax Whole or 1½-inch pieces	20-35	20-30
Broccoli Flowerets and stem Whole or 2-inch pieces	15-20	20-22
Brussels Sprouts	20-25	25-30
Carrots Sliced crosswise or quartered lengthwise	30-45	—
Cauliflower Flowerets	15-20	20-22
Corn Kernels	20-25	25-30
Eggplant Peeled and cut in 1-inch cubes	30-40	—
Mushrooms Whole or sliced	8-12	—
Peas Shelled	15-20	15-20
Peas and Carrots	—	15-20
Zucchini Sliced or quartered lengthwise	25-30	—

Pork Chops and Ribs
Cooking Chart
Charcoal or Gas Kettles

THICKNESS OF CHOPS	APPROXIMATE COOKING TIME
1 inch	12-15 minutes per side
1½ inch	18-20 minutes per side
2 inches	20-25 minutes per side
Back ribs	1½-2½ hours total
Spareribs	1 to 1¼ hours total
Country-style ribs	1½-2½ hours total

NOTE: If heat is too intense, chops will dry out. Spread coals as for Kebab cooking (see page 7).

Baked Ham
Cooking Chart · Charcoal or Gas Kettles

TYPE OF ROAST	INTERNAL TEMP.*	APPROX. MIN. PER LB.
Ham, fully cooked	140°	8-10
Ham, uncooked		
Whole (10-14 lbs.)	160°	10-15 ready to serve
Half (5-7 lbs.)	160°	12-18 ready to serve
Shank (3-4 lbs.)	160°	30-35 ready to serve
Rump (3-4 lbs.)	160°	30-35 ready to serve

Game

Cooking Chart • Charcoal or Gas Kettles

TYPE OF GAME	WEIGHT (POUNDS)	INTERNAL TEMP.	APPROX. MIN. PER LB.
NOTE: Game birds can dry out. Cover breasts with bacon slices.			
Duck, wild	1-1½	—	60-80
Goose, wild	6-8	—	20-25
Pheasant	2-3	—	25-35
Quail	individual	—	15-20 ready to serve
Squab	1¼	—	45-60 ready to serve
Venison Roast saddle Roast leg	6-7 6-7	140°-150° 140°-150°	25-30 25-30
Steaks	Use Beef Steak Chart, page 81, noting that all venison should be cooked rare.		
NOTE: Venison is often marinated for 24 hours before cooking.			

Poultry

Cooking Chart • Charcoal or Gas Kettles

TYPE OF POULTRY	WEIGHT (POUNDS)	INTERNAL TEMP.	APPROX. MIN. PER LB.
Capon	5-8	185°	15-20
Chicken	2½-3½	185°	18-20
Duck	4-6	185°	12-15
Duckling	5-6	185°	12-15
Goose	8-12	185°	30-35
Rock Cornish Hens	¾-1½	185°	45-60
Turkey	See chart, page 81.		

Turkey

Thawing Time Chart
Frozen Unstuffed Turkeys
or Turkey Rolls

TURKEY WEIGHT (POUNDS)	THAWED IN	IT WILL TAKE
8-12	Refrigerator	1 to 2 days
8-12	Cold water and refrigerator	8 to 10 hours in cold water to soften, then 4 to 6 hours in refrigerator.
12-20	Refrigerator	2 to 3 days

Poultry

Stuffing Chart

TYPE OF POULTRY	WEIGHT (POUNDS)	CUPS OF STUFFING
Capon	5-8	6
Chicken	4	4
Rock Cornish Hens	¾-1	¾-1 per hen
Duck	3½-5	4-5
Goose	10-12	10-12 (2½-3 quarts)
Turkey	7-8	8
	10-12	10-12 (2½-3 quarts)
	16	16
	20-24	20-24 (5-6 quarts)

Roast Beef

⅓ to ½ lb. boneless roast = 1 serving.
½ to 1 lb. bone-in roast = 1 serving.

What to Buy? Standing rib roast; Rolled rib roast; Rib eye (Delmonico) roast; Loin roast; Sirloin roast; and Tenderloin roast are "the" beef roasts. Best served rare. High-quality less expensive cuts that may be roasted are: Sirloin tip; Standing rump; Rolled rump. Best served medium rare, sliced thin.

To Prepare: Allow roast to stand at room temperature for 1½ to 2 hours. Wipe surface with a damp cloth. Season, if desired, with salt and pepper. Insert meat thermometer in center of largest lean muscle, not touching bone, fat or gristle.

To Serve: Remove roast from grill when desired internal temperature is reached; allow to stand for 20 to 30 minutes. The roast will be easier to carve and will continue cooking as much as 10° (even 15° in a large roast).

(1a)

Grilled Beef Steaks

⅓ to ½ lb. boneless steak = 1 serving.
¾ to 1 lb. bone-in steak = 1 serving.

What to Buy? Prime or Choice grade Porterhouse; Rib eye (Delmonico); Tenderloin; T-bone; Sirloin; Rib; and Club are the steaks preferred for grilling.

High-quality Chuck, Round and Flank steaks may also be grilled. The first two should be marinated or tenderized before cooking, and the last cooked very briefly. All should be served sliced thin. Buy steaks from 1 to 2 inches thick, well marbled with fat.

To Prepare: Trim fat to within ½ inch of meat and slash at 1½- to 2-inch intervals to prevent curling. Bring to room temperature. Rub with cut clove of garlic and sprinkle with pepper, if desired. Do not salt until halfway through or finished cooking so steak surface will remain dry for proper searing. Blot surfaces dry with paper before placing on grill.

To Serve: Serve "as is" with butter or with Béarnaise Sauce (page 53), Roquefort Sauce (page 55), Maître d'Hôtel Butter (page 13) or Mustard Butter (page 31).

(2a)

Grilled Beef Steak Cooking Chart

Be sure to preheat grill. For charcoal, grill by **Direct Heat Method,** turning steak halfway through cooking (follow Estimated Cooking Time below). For gas, sear steak for 1 minute on each side by **Direct Heat Method (High Heat)** with cover off. Move steak to edge of grill and continue cooking with cover on by **Indirect Heat Method (High Heat),** turning steak halfway through cooking (follow Estimated Cooking Time below). To check for doneness, slash steak in center (away from bone) and check color.

ESTIMATED COOKING TIME

DONENESS	MINUTES PER SIDE		
	1 Inch	1½ Inches	2 Inches
Rare	3-4	5-6	7-8
Medium Rare	4-5	7-8	8-9
Medium	5-6	8-9	9-10
Well Done	8+	10+	12+

Roast Beef Cooking Chart

Roast by **Indirect Heat Method** for charcoal, by **Indirect Heat Method (Low Heat)** for gas, with meat fat side up on the grill over a drip pan or, to protect the drippings and juices, on a rack in a close-fitting shallow pan on top of the grill. Add extra briquettes every hour (page 4).

TEMPERATURE WHEN REMOVED FROM GRILL

Rare ....120°	Medium Rare ....130°	
Medium .....140°	Well Done ....150°	

ESTIMATED COOKING TIME

TYPE OF ROAST	MINUTES PER POUND		
	Rare	Medium	Well Done
Rib (4-6 lbs.)	18-20	20-25	25-30
Rib (6-8 lbs.)	16-18	18-20	20-22
Rib Eye (4-6 lbs.)	16-18	18-20	20-22
Rolled Rump (4-6 lbs.) Internal Temp. 150°-170°			
	18-22		
Sirloin Tip (3½-4 lbs.) Internal Temp. 140°-170°			
	25-30		
Sirloin Tip (6-8 lbs.) Internal Temp. 140°-170°			
	20-25		
Tenderloin (4-6 lbs.)	40-60 Total		
Tenderloin (half)	40-60 Total		

Burgers

⅓ to ½ lb. ground meat = 1 dinner-size burger.
¼ to ⅓ lb. ground meat = 1 bun-size burger.

What to Buy? Prepackaged ground chuck (15% to 20% fat) is ideal. Or select lean beef and have the butcher coarse-grind it to order with 2 ounces beef suet to each pound of beef.

To Prepare: Handle the meat lightly and as little as possible. Do not pack. Make the patties ¾ to 1 inch thick. Season each pound of beef with 1 teaspoon salt and freshly ground pepper to taste.

To Season: For each pound of ground beef, add one or more of the following: ¼ cup sour cream; ½ cup grated cheese; ¼ to ½ cup finely chopped water chestnuts, green or ripe olives, green pepper, dill pickles, onions, scallions or chives; 1 to 2 tablespoons Worcestershire, soy or steak sauce; ½ to 1 teaspoon rosemary, thyme, oregano, basil or dry mustard.

(3a)

Meat Loaves and Seasoned Burgers

For Burgers: Season each pound chilled ground meat as indicated below.

For Meat Loaves: For each 1 lb. ground meat, add 1 beaten egg and 1 cup crumbs (bread, corn bread, crackers, chips); season as below. Pack in loaf pan or form in loaf shape and place in shallow pan.

Bacon-Cheese: ½ cup grated cheese, 1 minced small onion, ¼ cup crumbled cooked bacon, 1 teaspoon Worcestershire sauce.

Cheese-Nut: ¾ cup shredded Cheddar, ½ cup chopped walnuts, ¼ cup (1 tablespoon for burgers) red wine, 2 teaspoons Worcestershire sauce, 1 teaspoon each Dijon mustard and salt.

Chili: ¼ cup (1 tablespoon for burgers) chili sauce; 1 tablespoon each Worcestershire sauce, wine vinegar and grated onion; ½ teaspoon chili powder, 1 minced clove garlic.

Dill: ¼ cup (1 tablespoon for burgers) sour cream; 1 tablespoon each dried dillweed, chopped chives and capers; ½ teaspoon salt, pepper.

(4a)

Meat Loaves and Seasoned Burgers

See top of reverse side of card for meat loaf and burger instructions.

Italian Style: 1 cup grated mozzarella cheese, ¼ teaspoon oregano, 1 teaspoon salt, ¼ teaspoon pepper. Baste with tomato sauce.

Olive: ½ cup chopped olives, ¼ cup minced onion, salt and pepper to taste.

Grill Burgers according to instructions on Card 3a. Bake meat loaf by **Indirect Heat Method** for charcoal, by **Indirect Heat Method (Low Heat)** for gas.

ESTIMATED TOTAL COOKING TIME

LOAVES	INTERNAL TEMP.—170°
1 pound	40-50 minutes
1½ pounds	50-70 minutes
2 pounds	70-110 minutes

Grilled Burger Cooking Chart

Grill by **Direct Heat Method** for charcoal, by **Indirect Heat Method (High Heat)** for gas.

ESTIMATED COOKING TIME

THICKNESS	MINUTES PER SIDE		
	Rare	Medium	Well Done
¾ inch	3	4	5
1 inch	4-5	5-6	6-7

Burger Bastes (used throughout cooking): Soy, barbecue or Worcestershire sauce; Dijon mustard; Burgundy wine; Wine vinegar.

Serve Topped with: Chopped green or ripe olives; Sour cream; Cheddar, Swiss or Roquefort cheese; Sliced sautéed mushrooms; Sliced avocados; Fried or poached egg; Crumbled bacon; Raw or Grilled Onions (page 12); Guacamole (page 16); Horseradish; Smoky Barbecue (page 60), Honey-Soy Barbecue (page 59), Roquefort (page 55) or Béarnaise (page 53) Sauce; Mayonnaise; Dill pickle.

Burger Breads (brushed with melted butter and toasted lightly on edge of grill): Sesame buns; Onion, French or Italian rolls; English muffins; Rye or brown bread.

Baked Ham

¼ to ⅓ lb. boneless cooked ham = 1 serving.
⅓ to ½ lb. bone-in cooked ham = 1 serving.
⅓ to ½ lb. boneless uncooked ham = 1 serving.
½ to ¾ lb. bone-in uncooked ham = 1 serving.

What to Buy? Whole or half boneless or bone-in fully-cooked ham or cured and smoked uncooked ham.

To Prepare: Know whether ham needs full cooking or only heating by reading instructions on can or label or by asking butcher. When ready to bake, remove rind if necessary. Trim fat to within ½ inch; score and stud with cloves. Insert meat thermometer into thickest part of ham, not touching bone or fat.

Baked Ham Cooking Guide

Bake by **Indirect Heat Method** for charcoal, by **Indirect Heat Method (Low Heat)** for gas, fat side up, following Estimated Cooking Time on reverse of card. Baste for flavor throughout cooking if desired with ginger ale, a cola drink or fruit juice. Glaze (Card 16b) during last 30 minutes.

Roast Fresh Pork

⅓ lb. boneless fresh pork = 1 serving.
⅓ to ½ lb. bone-in fresh pork = 1 serving.
¾ to 1 lb. spareribs = 1 serving.

What to Buy? Boned or unboned: Loin; Center loin; Fresh ham; Picnic shoulder; Arm; Sirloin; Blade loin; Crown roast.

To Prepare: Season (see reverse side of card) several hours in advance. Allow to come to room temperature for 1½ to 2 hours. Insert meat thermometer into center of thickest muscle, not touching bone, fat or gristle.

Roast Fresh Pork Cooking Guide

Roast by **Indirect Heat Method** for charcoal, by **Indirect Heat Method (Low Heat)** for gas, with meat fat side up on grill over drip pan or, to protect drippings and juices, on rack in close-fitting shallow pan on top of grill. Estimate 20 minutes per pound. Add extra briquettes every hour (page 4).

To Serve: Remove roast when 160° internal temperature is reached and allow to stand for 20 to 30 minutes. Roast will be easier to carve and will continue cooking in its own heat.

Fresh Roast Pork Seasonings

Rub roast with salt, powdered bay leaf and powdered thyme. Baste with beer, cider or white wine.

Cut small, deep slits in roast 12 to 24 hours before roasting and stuff with sage leaves or dry sage. Rub with salt and powdered bay leaf; cover with minced garlic; refrigerate. Baste roast with French Vinaigrette Baste (Card 14a) several times during the cooking.

Cut small, deep slits in roast and stuff with slivers of garlic; spread surface of roast with prepared mustard. Sprinkle ¾ cup packed brown sugar over roast 30 minutes before cooking time is completed.

See cards 15a and 15b for additional bastes.

Baked Ham

ESTIMATED COOKING TIME

Fully cooked ham	8-10 minutes per lb.
Uncooked ham	10-15 minutes per lb.

INTERNAL TEMPERATURE

140° for fully cooked ham, 160° for uncooked ham

Carving

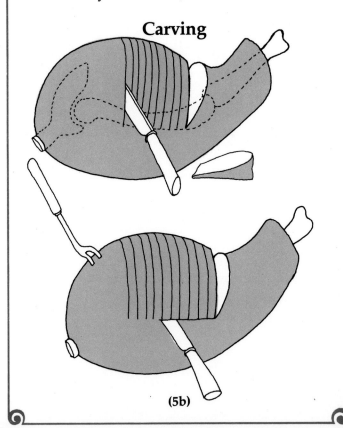

Pork Chops and Steaks

⅓ to ½ lb. boneless meat = 1 serving.
½ to ¾ lb. bone-in meat = 1 serving.

What to Buy? Center-cut rib or loin chops; Shoulder chops or steaks; Center-cut fresh ham. Have meat cut 1 to 1½ inches thick.

To Prepare: Wipe dry and season or let stand 30 minutes in a Baste/Marinade (Cards 14a-15b). Slash fat to prevent curling.

Pork Chop and Steak Cooking Chart

Grill by **Direct Heat Method** for charcoal, by **Indirect Heat Method (High Heat)** for gas. Follow **Special Kebab Instructions** (see page 7). Pork should be cooked thoroughly. To test for doneness, slash meat fairly close to bone; no pink should remain.

ESTIMATED COOKING TIME

THICKNESS	MINUTES PER SIDE
Fresh Loin or Rib Chops	
1 inch	15-18
1½ inches	18-20
Shoulder Chops or Steaks	
1 inch	10-15
1½ inches	15-20

Roast Lamb

½ lb. boneless leg or shoulder = 1 serving.
½ to ¾ lb. bone-in shoulder or leg = 1 serving.
1 or 2 rib or loin chops = 1 serving.

What to Buy? Leg; Shoulder; Rolled shoulder; Rib roast (rack); Double loin roast (saddle); Rib crown roast; Breast (bone-in or boneless rolled for stuffing).

To Prepare: Puncture meat all over with tip of knife; stuff slits with: Slivered garlic; Mint; Mixture of 2 slices minced bacon, 2 crushed cloves garlic, 2 minced scallions, 1 teaspoon thyme. Rub salt and pepper into meat. Or marinate for 12 to 24 hours in Red Wine Marinade (Card 15a). Allow roast to come to room temperature for 1½ to 2 hours. Insert meat thermometer into the center of the thickest muscle, not touching bone, gristle or fat. Stuff boneless roasts if desired (see Stuffed Lamb, page 29).

To Serve: Remove roast from grill when desired internal temperature is reached and allow to stand for 20 to 30 minutes. The roast will continue cooking in its own heat and be easier to carve.

Roast Lamb Cooking Chart

Roast by **Indirect Heat Method** for charcoal, by **Indirect Heat Method (Low Heat)** for gas, with meat fat side up on the grill over a drip pan or, to protect the drippings and juices, in a rack in a close-fitting shallow pan on top of the grill. Baste if desired (see Cards 14a-15b). See Briquette Chart (page 4) for adding coals.

INTERNAL TEMPERATURE
WHEN REMOVED FROM GRILL

Rare ....130°	**Medium Rare** .....140°	
Medium .....150°	**Well Done** ....160°	

ESTIMATED COOKING TIME

TYPE OF ROAST	MINUTES PER POUND		
	Rare	Med.	Well Done
Whole Leg (5-8 lbs.)	18-22	22-28	28-33
Half Leg (Shank)	22-28	28-33	33-38
Half Leg (Sirloin)	18-22	22-28	28-33
Boned Rolled Roast	22-28	28-33	33-38
Rib Roast (1½-2 lbs.)	30-35	35-40	40-45
Rib Roast (2-3 lbs.)	25-30	30-35	35-40
Rib Crown Roast (2½-4 lbs.)	28-33	33-38	38-43
Shoulder (Square cut)		22-28	28-35
Shoulder (Boneless)	28-33	33-38	38-43

Lamb Chops and Steaks

⅓ to ½ lb. boneless lamb = 1 serving.
¾ to 1 lb. bone-in lamb = 1 serving.

What to Buy? Center-cut loin or rib chops; Sirloin chops; Shoulder chops or steaks; Center-cut leg steaks. Have meat cut 1 to 2 inches thick.

To Prepare: Wipe dry and season; rub with crushed garlic and brush with olive oil if desired. Or let stand 30 minutes in a Baste/Marinade (Cards 14a-15b).

To Serve: Serve with Maître d'Hôtel Butter (page 13) or Mustard Butter (page 31).

Lamb Chop and Steak Cooking Chart

Grill by **Direct Heat Method** for charcoal, by **Indirect Heat Method (High Heat)** for gas.

ESTIMATED COOKING TIME

DONENESS	MINUTES PER SIDE		
	1 Inch	1½ Inches	2 Inches
Rare	5-6	7	8-9
Medium Rare	6-7	8	10-11
Medium	7	9	11-12
Well Done	8	10	12-14

Roast Chicken

1 squab chicken or Rock Cornish hen
(1 to 1¼ lbs.) = 1 to 2 servings.
1 broiler-fryer (2 to 3 lbs.) = 2 to 4 servings.
1 roaster (3 to 4 lbs.) = 4 to 5 servings.
1 capon (5 to 8 lbs.) = 6 to 10 servings.

What to Buy? Even Rock Cornish hens come fresh now, so try to buy a bird that has never seen a freezer. Select any of the above. A capon has a surplus benefit in its plump, tender breast.

To Prepare: Wipe the bird inside and out with a damp cloth and rub the cavity with a cut lemon to freshen. Sprinkle inside with salt and pepper and tuck the wings back. Allow to come to room temperature. If serving unstuffed, the cavity may be seasoned with 2 tablespoons butter and a selection of aromatic vegetables and herbs of your choice: Try crushed garlic cloves; Onion wedges; Chopped carrots; Celery stalk; Apple; Parsley; Rosemary; Tarragon; Thyme. The vent of stuffed birds may be sewed or skewered shut. Truss the bird tightly (page 36) and rub with 1 or 2 tablespoons softened butter. If self-basting is desired, lay slices of bacon across the bird.

(9a)

Barbecued Chicken

¾ to 1 lb. chicken = 1 serving.

What to Buy? Select whole, fresh (unfrozen) broilers or fryers (1½ to 3 pounds) and cut them yourself to save money and flavor.

To Prepare: Remove backbone and cut chicken into quarters or parts. Tuck wing tips back to form triangles. Wipe pieces with a damp cloth or quickly rinse and pat dry. Rub with softened butter or oil and season with salt and pepper. Add a sprinkling of crushed rosemary, tarragon, thyme, paprika, minced garlic or lemon juice, if desired. Or, marinate chicken in a Marinade/Baste (Cards 14a-15b).

Barbecued Chicken Cooking Guide

Grill by **Indirect Heat Method** for charcoal, by **Indirect Heat Method (Low Heat)** for gas. Turn and baste frequently. Use any desired glaze (Card 16a) or barbecue sauce during last 10 minutes of cooking. Chicken is done if juices run clear when meat is pierced with a skewer. Total estimated cooking time for charcoal and gas for parts, quarters and halves is 60 minutes.

(10a)

Poultry
Cutting and Boning

(10b)

Roast Chicken Cooking Chart

Roast by **Indirect Heat Method** for charcoal, by **Indirect Heat Method (Low Heat)** for gas, breast side up on the grill over a drip pan or, to protect drippings and juices, on a rack in a close-fitting shallow pan on top of grill. If bacon is not used, baste every 15 minutes with butter or a basting sauce (see Cards 14a-15b). Bird is done when the leg can be moved easily or if juices run clear when thigh is pierced with a skewer.

ESTIMATED TOTAL COOKING TIME

Add an extra 15 minutes if chicken is stuffed.

Squab chicken or Rock Cornish hen (¾ to 1¼ lbs.)	1 hr. 15 min.
Broiler-fryer (2 to 3 lbs.)	1 hr. 10-20 min.
Roaster (3 to 4 lbs.)	1 hr. 30-45 min.
Capon (5 to 8 lbs.)	2-2½ hrs.

To Serve: Allow large birds to stand for 10 to 15 minutes before carving. Serve small birds as soon as possible, whole or cut into serving pieces.

(9b)

Roast Turkey

¾ to 1 lb. turkey under 12 lbs. = 1 serving.
½ to ¾ lb. turkey over 12 lbs. = 1 serving.

What to Buy? Turkeys come fresh, frozen and self-basting. Purchase frozen turkey early enough to thaw in refrigerator.

To Prepare: See Roast Chicken (Card 9). When the bird is trussed, rub with peanut oil. Insert meat thermometer in center of inside thigh muscle.

Roast Turkey Cooking Chart

Roast by **Indirect Heat Method** for charcoal, by **Indirect Heat Method (Low Heat)** for gas, breast side up. Baste frequently. Roast to internal temperature of 180°. Allow to stand 20 minutes before carving.

ESTIMATED TOTAL COOKING TIME

For stuffed turkey, allow 13 minutes per pound.

FRESH OR FROZEN, THAWED	INTERNAL TEMP.	TIME
6-8 lbs.	185°	2 to 2¾ hrs.
8-12 lbs.	185°	2½ to 3¾ hrs.
12-16 lbs.	185°	3½ to 4 hrs.
16-20 lbs.	185°	4½ to 5 hrs.

(11a)

Grilled Fish

1 lb. dressed fish = 1 serving.
½ to ¾ lb. fish steak = 1 serving.

What to Buy? Whole pan fish; Split larger (3 to 5 lbs.) fish; Fish steaks (1 to 2 inches), preferably cut from tail.

To Prepare: Pat dry, brush with butter or oil and season. Use a well-greased, preheated grill and have on hand 2 large, broad spatulas for aid in turning.

Grilled Fish Cooking Guide

Grill by **Direct Heat Method** for charcoal, by **Indirect Heat Method (Low Heat)** for gas. Arrange firebed as you would for **Kebab** cooking. See page 7. Baste every few minutes with butter, oil or a Marinade/Baste (Cards 14a-15b). Estimate 10 to 15 minutes per pound cooking time, keeping in mind that thickness rather than weight determines total time. Fish is done when flesh flakes easily with a fork.

(12a)

Baked Fish

1 lb. dressed fish = 1 serving.
½ to ¾ lb. fish steak = 1 serving.
⅓ to ½ fillet = 1 serving.

What to Buy? Whole fish, small or large; Steaks; Fillets.

To Prepare: Pat dry with paper toweling and brush with melted butter, oil or a Marinade/Baste (Cards 14a-15b). Line cavity of whole fish with thin slices of lemon and/or onion, or stuff. Grease an aluminum foil pan or make a bed of chopped carrots, onion and celery dotted with butter in it. Place fish in pan and add about ¼ cup liquid (lemon juice, wine, water).

Bake by **Indirect Heat Method** for charcoal, by **Indirect Heat Method (Low Heat)** for gas.

ESTIMATED COOKING TIME

Large whole fish	**8-10 minutes per lb.**
Pan fish	**12-20 minutes total**
Steaks (1 to 2 inches)	**10-20 minutes total**
Fillets	**10 minutes total**

Remember, a long thin fish will cook faster than a thicker fish of the same weight.

Roast Duck

1 duck (3½ lbs.) = 2 servings.
1 duck (4½ lbs.) = 3 servings.
1 duck (5½ lbs.) = 4 servings.

To Prepare: Remove any fat from the cavity and sprinkle with salt and pepper. If not stuffing the duck, celery or sliced onions or apples may be placed in the cavity. Sew or skewer vent shut and truss (page 36). Prick skin of the duck around the back and the base of the thighs and breast. Rub with salt.

Roast Duck Cooking Chart

Roast by **Indirect Heat Method** for charcoal, by **Indirect Heat Method (Low Heat)** for gas. For a crisp skin, baste during last 15 minutes with ice water, orange juice or a Glaze for Poultry (Card 16a). Bird is done when breast is soft to touch and meat still rosy near thigh bone.

ESTIMATED TOTAL COOKING TIME

Add a total of 20 to 30 minutes if duck is stuffed.

FRESH OR FROZEN, THAWED	TIME
3½ lbs.	1½ to 2 hrs.
4½ lbs.	2 to 2½ hrs.
5½ lbs.	2½ to 3 hrs.

Broiled Lobster

1 lobster (1 lb.) = 1 serving.

To Prepare: Kill lobster (page 51).

Grill by **Direct Heat Method** for charcoal, by **Indirect Heat Method (High Heat)** for gas, shell side up. Cook for 15 to 20 minutes or until shell is bright red.

To Serve: Split in half lengthwise. Remove stomach and intestinal vein (page 51).

Lobster Tails

1 to 2 tails (8 oz. each) = 1 serving.

To Prepare: Thaw the tails. Cut away thin undershell and flippers with kitchen shears. Bend tail backward until it cracks. Brush with melted butter.

Grill by **Direct Heat Method** for charcoal, by **Indirect Heat Method (High Heat)** for gas, meat side down for 3 to 4 minutes. Turn and baste with melted butter. Cook 7 to 10 minutes more or until shell is bright red.

Marinades/Bastes

Use throughout cooking (except for Beer Baste).

Beer Baste: ½ cup beer, ⅓ cup firmly packed brown sugar, 2 tablespoons each vinegar and honey, ⅔ cup chili sauce, 1 tablespoon each Worcestershire sauce and lemon juice. Use during last hour. *For baked ham.*

Currant Jelly Baste: 1 cup melted currant jelly, ½ cup orange juice, 1 tablespoon grated orange peel. *For lamb, duck.*

French Vinaigrette Marinade/Baste: ½ cup olive or peanut oil, 2 tablespoons wine vinegar, ½ teaspoon dry mustard, ½ teaspoon salt, pepper. *For poultry, lamb, pork.*

Ginger–Curry Butter Baste: ½ cup melted butter, 3 tablespoons drained chopped preserved ginger, 1 tablespoon ginger syrup, 1 tablespoon soy sauce, ½ teaspoon curry powder. *For pork, ham, poultry, lamb.*

Italian Oil Marinade/Baste: ½ cup olive oil, 2 to 3 tablespoons wine vinegar, 3 chopped scallions, 1½ teaspoons tarragon, ½ teaspoon salt, pepper. *For beef, poultry, lamb, fish.*

Marinades/Bastes

Use throughout cooking.

Lebanese Garlic Marinade/Baste: ½ cup olive oil, 3 cloves garlic, crushed, 1 tablespoon lemon juice, ½ teaspoon salt, pepper. *For poultry, lamb, fish.*

Lemon–Garlic Butter Baste: ¼ cup melted butter, 2 cloves garlic, crushed. Allow to stand 30 minutes. Add juice of 1 lemon, ½ teaspoon salt. *For poultry, fish, lamb.*

Lemon–Parsley Butter Baste: ¼ cup melted butter, juice of ½ lemon, 1 tablespoon chopped parsley, ½ teaspoon salt, pepper. *For fish, poultry.*

Mint Jelly Baste: 1 cup melted mint jelly, ¼ cup lemon juice, 1 tablespoon grated lemon rind. *For lamb.*

Olive Oil Marinade/Baste: Begin with ½ cup olive oil, juice of 1 small lemon, ½ teaspoon salt, pepper. Add one or more of following: 1 clove garlic, crushed; 1 small onion, sliced; 1 bay leaf; 1 teaspoon tarragon, basil or dillweed; 1 tablespoon tomato puree, soy sauce or Worcestershire sauce. *For fish, poultry, lamb, beef.*

(14b)

Shrimp

2 lbs. = 4 entree servings or 6 to 8 appetizer servings.

To Prepare: Shell and devein shrimp. Place in a buttered heavy-duty aluminum foil pan with 3 tablespoons water, 4 peppercorns, 1 bay leaf and 1 rib celery; seal. Or, skewer shrimp and brush with melted butter.

Cook by **Direct Heat Method** for charcoal, by **Indirect Heat Method (High Heat)** for gas, 10 minutes for foil packet, 6 to 8 minutes for skewers, or until shrimp are just pink.

Do not overcook. Shrimp will become tough and rubbery if cooked longer than necessary.

Alaska King Crab Legs

1 lb. frozen legs = 1 serving.

To Prepare: Thaw and spread meat with softened butter on split side.

Grill by **Direct Heat Method** for charcoal, by **Indirect Heat Method (High Heat)** for gas, cut side up, only until heated through.

(13b)

Marinades/Bastes

Use throughout cooking.

Onion–Bacon Baste: Sauté 3 slices minced bacon and ⅓ cup minced onion until lightly browned. Add ⅓ cup melted butter. *For poultry.*

Orange Baste: 1 cup orange juice, ½ cup sherry or grenadine. *For baked ham.*

Pineapple Baste: 1 cup pineapple juice, ½ cup sherry or grenadine. *For baked ham.*

Rosemary Butter Baste: ½ cup melted butter, juice of 1 lemon, 1 tablespoon crushed rosemary. *For poultry, lamb.*

Red Wine Marinade: 2 cups red wine, ½ cup olive oil, 1 sliced onion, 2 tablespoons chopped parsley, 2 tablespoons rosemary, ¼ teaspoon ground cloves. Marinate 12 to 24 hours. *For lamb, beef.*

Soy Marinade/Baste: ½ cup peanut oil, ⅓ cup soy sauce, 2 tablespoons brown sugar, 1 tablespoon wine vinegar, ½ teaspoon grated gingerroot, 1 clove garlic, crushed. *For fish, pork, poultry.*

(15a)

Glazes for Poultry

Use only during last 10-15 minutes cooking.

Mustard–Honey Glaze: ¼ cup honey, 2 tablespoons Dijon mustard, 2 tablespoons lemon juice, ½ teaspoon salt.

Oriental Orange Glaze: ¼ cup melted butter, ½ cup orange marmalade, ½ teaspoon grated gingerroot, 1 teaspoon grated orange rind.

Peach–Brandy Glaze: ¼ cup melted butter, 2 tablespoons lemon juice, 2 tablespoons brown sugar, 2 tablespoons peach nectar, 2 tablespoons brandy.

Soy–Honey Glaze: 2 tablespoons melted butter, ¼ cup honey, 2 tablespoons lemon juice, 2 tablespoons soy sauce.

Spicy Plum Glaze: 1 cup red plum preserves, 2 teaspoons brown sugar, 2 teaspoons red wine vinegar, ½ cup mango chutney. Leftover glaze may be served as a sauce.

Sweet-and-Sour Apricot Glaze: ½ cup apricot preserves (chop any large lumps), 3 to 4 tablespoons wine vinegar.

(16a)

Glazes for Baked Ham

Use during last 30 minutes of cooking.

Apricot Glaze: Spread ham with ½ cup apricot preserves. If desired, sprinkle with julienne strips of dried apricots softened in hot rum or cider.

Brown Sugar Glaze: Blend 1 cup firmly packed brown sugar with 1 to 2 teaspoons dry mustard. Stir in ½ cup beer, cider or pineapple, orange or cranberry juice.

Crunchy Peanut Glaze: Spread ham with 1½ cups creamy or chunky peanut butter blended with ¼ cup honey.

Mustard–Honey Glaze: Spread ham with ¾ cup prepared mustard, sprinkle with ¾ cup brown sugar and drizzle with 3 to 4 tablespoons honey.

Orange Glaze: Combine 1 cup firmly packed brown sugar, 1 cup orange juice, 1 tablespoon grated orange peel.

Spiced Glaze: Add ¼ teaspoon each ground cinnamon, allspice and cloves to Brown Sugar Glaze (above).

Marinades/Bastes

Use throughout cooking.

Soy–Honey Marinade/Baste: ½ cup each soy sauce, honey and water; ¼ cup dry sherry; 2 tablespoons sugar; 1 teaspoon minced gingerroot; 2 cloves garlic, crushed; 1 teaspoon dry mustard; 1 teaspoon salt; ¼ teaspoon pepper. Marinate 12 to 24 hours. *For pork.*

Soy–Lemon Marinade/Baste: ½ cup olive or peanut oil, ¼ cup soy sauce, juice of 1 lemon, 2 cloves garlic, minced. *For broiled beef, poultry, pork, fish.*

Tarragon Butter Baste: ½ cup melted butter, juice of 1 lemon, 1 tablespoon crushed tarragon. *For poultry, fish.*

White Wine Marinade: ½ cup dry white wine, 2 tablespoons salad oil, 4 thin slices onion, 1 teaspoon Worcestershire sauce, ¼ teaspoon salt, 4 peppercorns. *For fish.*

Wine Butter Baste: ¼ cup melted butter, ¼ cup very dry white wine, ½ teaspoon salt, ⅛ teaspoon paprika. *For poultry, fish.*

Vegetables in Foil

General Instructions: Center from 1 to 3 servings of prepared vegetable in a square of buttered heavy-duty aluminum foil. Season; seal, leaving space for steam expansion. Cook by **Indirect Heat Method** for charcoal, by **Indirect Heat Method (Low Heat)** for gas.

Acorn Squash (page 76)

Artichoke, whole   **60 minutes**
Cut off stem and trim leaves with scissors. 1 per packet with 3 tablespoons water. When done, leaves will pull out easily. Serve hot with melted butter or Hollandaise Sauce (page 53), or cold with Mustard Mayonnaise (page 54).

Artichoke Hearts (page 74)

Asparagus   **10 to 20 minutes**
Whole or cut diagonally into pieces. 2 tablespoons water and a dash of nutmeg; dot with butter. Check cooking early. Serve with Lemon Butter (page 50) or Hollandaise Sauce (page 53).

Vegetables in Foil

See General Instructions, Card 17a.

Carrots   **30 to 45 minutes**
Whole if tiny, peeled and in strips if large. Add 1 tablespoon water and dot with butter. When tender, serve with butter, chopped chives and dillweed. See also Sweet Glazed Carrots (page 77).

Cauliflower   **15 to 20 minutes**
Break into cauliflowerets. Add 1 tablespoon water; salt and dot with butter. When just tender, serve with melted butter, Hollandaise Sauce (page 53) or a cheese sauce.

Celery   **10 to 15 minutes**
Peel away strings; cut into 1- to 2-inch pieces. Soak 30 minutes in salted water. Add 1 tablespoon water or beef stock per packet and dot with butter. Serve with melted butter, Hollandaise Sauce (page 53) or Sweet-and-Sour Sauce (page 56).

Corn on the Cob   **10 to 20 minutes**
Strip the corn husk and silk. Rub with softened butter. 1 per packet. See also Roast Corn (Card 19b).

Vegetables in Foil

See General Instructions, Card 17a.

Cucumbers　　　　　**12 to 15 minutes**
Peel, split lengthwise, remove seeds and cut in strips; salt and let stand 30 minutes. Drain; dot with butter. If desired add for each cucumber 1 slice chopped bacon and 2 tablespoons chopped onion; drain before adding to packet.

Eggplant (small)　　　　**30 to 40 minutes**
Peel and cut into 1-inch cubes. Salt, weight and let stand 30 minutes. Dot with butter. Or, toss cubes in mixture of ¼ cup olive oil, 2 tablespoons wine vinegar, 1 minced clove garlic, 2 tablespoons chopped parsley, ¼ teaspoon oregano, salt and pepper to taste.

Green Beans　　　　**20 to 35 minutes**
Leave whole or cut into pieces; season with salt and pepper and dot with butter. Or, for 1 pound raw beans, toss with 4 to 5 slices chopped bacon cooked with ¼ cup chopped onion and ¼ cup cider vinegar and 1½ tablespoons sugar.

Mushrooms (page 71)

Vegetables in Foil

See General Instructions, reverse side.

Beans (see Green Beans, Card 18b).

Beets (2-inch diameter)　　**30 to 40 minutes**
Trim tops 2 in. from beet; do not trim taproot. 4 to 6 per packet with 2 tablespoons water, ½ teaspoon salt. When tender, trim stems and slip off skins. Serve whole or sliced, with butter or sour cream and chopped chives.

Broccoli　　　　**15 to 20 minutes**
Trim base and peel stems to within 2 inches of tops; split stalks so all are about 1-inch thick. Add 2 tablespoons water per packet and dot with butter. When tender, serve with melted butter, Lemon Butter (page 50) or Hollandaise Sauce (page 53).

Brussels Sprouts　　　**20 to 25 minutes**
Trim stems; cut a ¼-inch cross in stem end. Add 2 tablespoons water or beef stock per packet and dot with butter.

Cabbage　　　　**15 to 20 minutes**
Shred cabbage; soak 30 minutes in ice water. Dot with butter or bacon fat. See also Bacon and Cabbage (page 65).

Vegetables in Foil

See General Instructions, Card 17a.

Onions (large)　　　　**45 to 60 minutes**
Peel and cut a deep cross in stem end. Push butter into the cross. 1 per packet with 1 teaspoon Worcestershire sauce. When tender, serve whole or chopped, with butter and a little cream.

Peas　　　　**15 to 20 minutes**
Shell just before cooking. 1 tablespoon water per packet and dot with butter; if desired add mint leaves or finely chopped ham sautéed with chopped scallions.

Peppers, Sweet　　　　**15 to 20 minutes**
Remove seeds and cut in strips. 1 tablespoon butter or olive oil per packet; if desired add 1 clove garlic, crushed.

Potatoes　　　　**45 to 60 minutes**
Scrub or peel and cut through at 1-inch intervals. Re-form each potato with butter between slices and if desired ½-inch onion slices. 1 per packet. When tender, serve with crumbled bacon, chopped chives and parsley or a dill–sour cream sauce.

Baked Fruit

General Instructions: Unless otherwise indicated, center from 1 to 3 servings of prepared fruit in a square of buttered heavy-duty aluminum foil. Flavor; seal, leaving space for steam expansion. Cook by **Indirect Heat Method** for charcoal, by **Indirect Heat Method (Low Heat)** for gas.

Apples　　　　**30 to 40 minutes**
Core, leaving ½-inch wall at bottom. Stuff with brown sugar, mincemeat or raisins, and nuts sprinkled with brown sugar and cinnamon; dot with butter. 1 per packet. When tender, serve with heavy or whipped cream.

Apricots　　　　**30 minutes**
Peel and pit. Sprinkle with lemon juice, brown sugar or honey, cinnamon and nutmeg; dot with butter. When tender, sprinkle with brandy or rum and serve with vanilla ice cream.

Bananas　　　　**10 to 15 minutes**
Peel and halve. Place on a large square of heavy-duty aluminum foil. Sprinkle with lemon juice and add 1 tablespoon each brown sugar and chopped walnuts for each banana. Seal the packet.

Baked Fruit

See General Instructions on reverse side.

Fruit Kabobs: Cut fruits of your choice into bite-size chunks; skewer. Brush with lemon juice; roll in brown sugar. Cook by **Direct Heat Method** for charcoal, by **Indirect Heat Method (High Heat)** for gas, until lightly browned. Baste with a mixture of 2 parts butter to 1 part rum. Serve with whipped cream.

Grapefruit   **30 to 45 minutes**
Halve; separate segments with knife. Drizzle with honey or grenadine or sprinkle with sugar; dot with butter. Bake in foil pan.

Oranges: Peel and halve. Treat as Grapefruit, above.

Peaches: Peel and pit. Treat as Apricots, reverse side.

Pears: Peel and core. Treat as Apricots, reverse side.

Pineapple   **30 to 40 minutes**
Quarter lengthwise, peel and core. Sprinkle with honey or brown sugar and rum; dot with butter. Bake in foil pan; baste with juices. Serve with whipped cream.

Vegetables in Foil

See General Instructions, Card 17a.

Roast Corn
Peel the husks from each ear halfway down and remove silk; fold husks back up. Soak ears several hours in cold water. Grill by **Direct Heat Method** for charcoal, by **Indirect Heat Method (High Heat)** for gas, for about 15 minutes or until kernels are tender when pressed. Wear heavy gloves to remove husks.

Sweet Potatoes and Yams   **45 to 60 minutes**
Scrub or peel potatoes; cut in ½-inch slices. Dot with butter; 1 per packet. If desired, add 2 tablespoons each crushed pineapple and miniature marshmallows and 1 tablespoon each dark brown sugar and rum. See also Banana-Stuffed Sweet Potatoes (page 76).

Zucchini   **20 to 25 minutes**
Scrub. Split lengthwise or slice. Dot with butter or add per packet 1 tablespoon olive oil and a sprinkling of oregano or basil, 1 clove garlic, crushed, and chopped tomato.